150 best Indian,
Thai, Vietnamese
& more Slow
Cooker
recipes

150 best Indian, Thai, Vietnamese & more Slow Cooker recipes

Sunil Vijayakar

Robert
ROSE

150 Best Indian, Thai, Vietnamese & More Slow Cooker Recipes
Text copyright © 2012 Octopus Publishing Group Ltd. and Robert Rose Inc.
First published in 2010 under the title SLOW COOKER CURRIES, by Hamlyn, in imprint of Octopus
    Publishing Group Ltd. Endeavour House, 189 Shaftsbury Avenue, London, WC2H 85Y. This version
    has been adapted to meet North American requirements.
Cover photograph copyright © 2012 Robert Rose Inc.
Cover and text design copyright © 2012 Robert Rose Inc.

Interior photographs: Sindhi Beef Curry, Cambodian Pork & Lemongrass Curry, Bombay Curry Chicken,
    Goan Xacutti Curry, Tomato-Based Vegetable Curry and Beet Curry by Colin Ericson, copyright ©
    Robert Rose Inc. • Bombay Aloo by Mark T. Shapiro, copyright © Robert Rose Inc. • Lamb-Spiked
    Mulligatawny Soup © iStock/Lulu Durand; Butter Chicken © iStock/travellinglight; Thai Green Chicken
    Curry © iStock/ShutterWorx; Channa Masala © iStock/Lauri Patterson; Chile & Tomato Chutney ©
    iStock/C. Gissemann; naan © iStock/Elizabeth Shoemaker; ground chiles with spoon © iStock/Evgenij
    Mymrin; spices © iStock/Surakit Harntongkul • Spiced Chickpea Curry © Fotosearch.com

For complete cataloguing information, see page 184.

Disclaimer
The recipes in this book have been carefully tested by our kitchen and our tasters. To the best of our
knowledge, they are safe and nutritious for ordinary use and users. For those people with food or other
allergies, or who have special food requirements or health issues, please read the suggested contents of
each recipe carefully and determine whether or not they may create a problem for you. All recipes are
used at the risk of the consumer.
    We cannot be responsible for any hazards, loss or damage that may occur as a result of any recipe use.
    For those with special needs, allergies, requirements or health problems, in the event of any doubt,
please contact your medical adviser prior to the use of any recipe.

Design and Production: Daniella Zanchetta/PageWave Graphics Inc.
Editor: Judith Finlayson
Recipe tester: Jennifer MacKenzie
Proofreader: Gillian Watts
Indexer: Gillian Watts
Photographer (cover): Colin Ericson
Associate Photographer (cover): Matt Johannsson
Food Stylist (cover): Kathryn Robertson
Prop Stylist (cover): Charlene Ericson

Cover image: Cambodian Pork & Lemongrass Curry (page 23)

We acknowledge the financial support of the Government of Canada through the Book Publishing Industry
Development Program (BPIDP) for our publishing activities.

Published by Robert Rose Inc.
120 Eglinton Avenue East, Suite 800, Toronto, Ontario, Canada M4P 1E2
Tel: (416) 322-6552 Fax: (416) 322-6936
www.robertrose.ca

Printed and bound in Canada

2 3 4 5 6 7 8 9 FP 20 19 18 17 16 15 14 13 12

Contents

Introduction

If you're a fan of the cuisines of India and Southeast Asia, then you'll be delighted to know that your slow cooker is the perfect appliance in which to cook many of the signature dishes from countries such as India, Thailand, Sri Lanka, Bangladesh, Indonesia, Malaysia, Burma (Myanmar) and other South Asian and Southeast Asian countries.

Many of the dishes from these countries are built around essential blends of spices and herbs. Typically, dishes such as Creamy Lamb Korma (page 35), Cambodian Pork & Lemongrass Curry (page 23) and Bombay Aloo (page 126) release their spectacular flavors gradually with the encouragement of low, steady heat. What better tool than the slow cooker to prepare them? Long, slow cooking allows spices to release their essential oils. Meat becomes beautifully tender and vegetables absorb tasty zing and zest.

What's more, a slow cooker will make your life easier. Spending as little as 15 to 20 minutes early in the day is often all it takes to prepare a slow cooker supper. Once the ingredients are in the slow cooker, you're free to get on with other things. Because the appliance has a lid that fits snugly and the food cooks so slowly, you don't need to worry about it boiling dry, spilling over or burning on the bottom.

A slow cooker is environmentally friendly, too. There is no need to turn on the oven to cook just one dish, and the appliance is very energy-efficient — it uses about the same amount of energy as a standard light bulb.

Although the cuisines represented in this book tend to be spicy, I've tried to include recipes to suit every palate. Look for the heat rating that accompanies every recipe: it will tell you whether the recipe will produce a dish that is hot or mild. Three flames indicate that it's very hot, one means that it's mild, and two signals in-between. Tips for adjusting the heat level are included in many of the recipes.

Unless specified, ingredients are assumed to be fresh. Most, including the prepared curry pastes, can be purchased at well-stocked supermarkets or Asian markets. If you live in a less urban area, they can certainly be found online.

With this book you can use your slow cooker to recreate at home dishes that you may have been able to enjoy only in restaurants. Even better, with the help of this amazing appliance, you can produce splendid results with a minimum of effort.

– Sunil Vijayakar

Slow Cooker Know-How

Although slow cookers are very easy to use, be sure to read carefully the booklet that accompanies your appliance, or visit the manufacturer's website for detailed instructions on its use.

Choose the Right Slow Cooker for You

When purchasing a slow cooker, choose one that has an indicator light so you can see at a glance when it is turned on. If you are likely to be away from the house for extended periods while your slow cooker is working, purchase a model with a timer — it will automatically switch to the Warm setting once the food has finished cooking. Cooked food can be held on Warm for up to two hours.

Size Matters

Slow cookers are round or oval in shape and range in size from $1\frac{1}{2}$ to 8 quarts. The size you buy should be based on the number of people you will likely be cooking for and the kind of recipes you intend to prepare.

The following guidelines will help you achieve the best results when making the recipes in this book:

- For two people, use a small slow cooker with a capacity of about 2 quarts ($1\frac{1}{2}$ to 3 quarts.)
- For four people, you'll want a medium-sized slow cooker about 4 quarts ($3\frac{1}{2}$ to 5 quarts) in capacity.
- For six or more people, you'll likely need a large slow cooker with a capacity of about 5 quarts.

Recipe yields (number of servings) and slow cooker size have been included for all recipes. Most of the recipes in this book have been tested in four-portion quantities in a 4-quart slow cooker. You can easily adjust the recipes to make a smaller or larger amount. Halve the recipe to make two portions or add half as much again to produce six portions. Just be sure to adjust the size of your slow cooker accordingly (see above.) Timing stays the same, regardless of the quantity you are preparing.

Size matters because the stoneware should be from at least one-third to three-quarters full. In any case, make sure the liquid comes to no higher than an inch (2.5 cm) from the top of the stoneware.

Using Your Slow Cooker

Before you actually start to cook, place the slow cooker on a work surface out of the way. The outside does get hot, so warn family members not to touch. Be sure to use oven mitts when removing the stoneware insert from the casing.

The insert is quite easy to clean. Allow it to cool, then fill with hot, soapy water and set aside to soak for a while before washing. If your dishwasher will accommodate it, most are dishwasher-safe.

Wipe the inside of the casing with a damp cloth and remove any stubborn marks with a gentle cleanser. Wipe the outside with a damp cloth. If you're storing the slow cooker in a cupboard, make sure it's completely cool before you put it away.

Heat Settings

There are two heat settings you will use to cook the recipes in this book: High and Low. When set to High, the appliance should cook at a temperature of roughly 300°F (150°C). On Low, the temperature will be about 200°F (100°C). In general terms, use the Low setting if you plan to be out of the house all day. Meat dishes will take about 8 hours to cook. If you're in a hurry, use the High setting, which produces similar results in about half that time. When appropriate (for instance, when cooking rice, fish or seafood or making chutney), a specific temperature setting has been recommended.

Know Your Slow Cooker
Be aware that cooking times vary among slow cookers. Some cook faster than others on the same setting. Try a few recipes in this book. If you find that your food is over- or undercooked, adjust the cooking times to suit your appliance.

Preparing Food for the Slow Cooker

Meat: If using frozen meat, thaw completely before using. Cut meat into equal-sized pieces to ensure even cooking. For best results, most meats are browned before being added to the slow cooker.

Vegetables: Surprisingly, some root vegetables (potatoes in particular) take longer to cook than meat. That's why it's important to cut them into small pieces. As with meat, cutting vegetables into evenly sized pieces helps to ensure even cooking. Some delicate or leafy vegetables, such as spinach and fresh peppers, do not benefit from long, slow cooking. They should be added only during the last 15 or 20 minutes of cooking.

Fish and Shellfish: Never add frozen product to the slow cooker. Thaw, rinse with cold water and drain well before use. When cooking fish, take care to ensure that it is covered by the hot liquid so that it cooks evenly right through to the center.

Rice: Parboiled (converted) rice is your best bet in the slow cooker because it has been partially cooked during the manufacturing process, which makes it less sticky.

Dried Legumes and Grains: For best results, soak dried beans in plenty of cold water overnight. Drain well, place in a saucepan with fresh cold water and boil rapidly for 10 minutes. Drain, reserving some (or all) of the cooking water (you may want to add it to your recipe for added flavor and nutrients). Lentils and grains such as pearled barley do not need to be soaked overnight.

Dairy Products: If you're using dairy products in a recipe, they are usually not added at the outset, because they are likely to sour during the slow cooking process. For best results, use full-fat dairy products, which are less likely to separate than lower-fat versions.

Meat Dishes

Beef Madras

Tips

Serve this curry with plenty of basmati rice to soak up the luscious sauce.

Madras curry powder, which usually contains dry curry leaves, tends to be on the hot side. Depending upon the heat level of your curry powder, this quantity may produce a spicy result. If you're heat-averse, use less.

For this quantity of tomatoes, use about half a standard small can (14 oz/398 mL) of diced tomatoes.

If you're using canned coconut milk, you can substitute one 14-oz (400 mL) can for this quantity. Be sure to shake well before using, because the cream layer collects at the top after it's been sitting.

To serve two people: Cut the quantities in half and use a small (approx. 2 quart) slow cooker.

To serve six people: Increase the quantities by half and use a large (approx. 5 quart) slow cooker.

Preparation Time: 15 minutes, plus marinating
Medium (approx. 4 quart) slow cooker
Heat Rating: ♨♨♨

¼ cup	plain yogurt (not lower-fat)	60 mL
¼ cup	Madras curry powder (see Tips, left)	60 mL
1¼ lbs	trimmed stewing beef, cut into 1-inch (2.5 cm) cubes	625 g
2 tbsp	oil	30 mL
1	large onion, halved and thinly sliced	1
3	cloves garlic, minced	3
2 tsp	minced gingerroot	10 mL
1 cup	diced tomatoes with juice (see Tips, left)	250 mL
2 cups	coconut milk (see Tips, left)	500 mL
¼ tsp	garam masala	1 mL
	Salt	
	Finely chopped cilantro leaves	

1. In a small bowl combine yogurt and curry powder. Place beef in a non-reactive bowl and add yogurt mixture. Toss to coat thoroughly. Cover and refrigerate for 24 hours.

2. In a large skillet or wok, heat oil over medium heat. Add onion and stir-fry until softened, about 4 minutes. Add garlic and ginger and stir-fry for 30 seconds. Reduce heat to low. Add beef with marinade and stir-fry until well coated with seasonings and beef begins to brown, about 6 minutes. Add tomatoes, coconut milk and garam masala and stir-fry for 1 minute, scraping up brown bits from bottom of pan.

3. Transfer to slow cooker stoneware. Season to taste with salt. Cover and cook on Low for 6 hours or on High for 3 hours, until beef is meltingly tender. Serve immediately, garnished with cilantro.

Sindhi Beef Curry

Tips

This simple curry is particularly delicious with a rice pilaf.

Add some Indian pickles for a finishing touch.

Preparation Time: 15 minutes
Medium (approx. 4 quart) slow cooker
Heat Rating:

2 lbs	trimmed stewing beef, cut into 1-inch (2.5 cm) cubes	1 kg
2 tbsp	curry powder	30 mL
1 tbsp	ground cardamom	15 mL
1 tsp	ground cinnamon	5 mL
¼ tsp	ground cloves	1 mL
4	large tomatoes, roughly chopped	4
2	red onions, finely chopped	2
¼ cup	tomato paste	60 mL
2 tsp	garam masala	10 mL
2 cups	water or beef broth	500 mL
	Salt and freshly ground black pepper	

1. In slow cooker stoneware, combine beef, curry powder, cardamom, cinnamon and cloves. Mix well.

2. Add tomatoes, onions, tomato paste, garam masala and water. Stir well and season to taste with salt and freshly ground black pepper. Cover and cook on Low for 8 hours or on High for 4 hours, until meat is meltingly tender.

Creamy Beef Curry

Serves 4

Tips

Serve this over a large mound of steaming basmati rice.

For a particularly Indian touch, use mustard oil.

To serve two people: Cut the quantities in half and use a small (approx. 2 quart) slow cooker.

To serve six people: Increase the quantities by half and use a large (approx. 5 quart) slow cooker.

Preparation Time: 20 minutes, plus marinating
Medium (approx. 4 quart) slow cooker
Heat Rating: ♦♦♦

⅓ cup	plain yogurt (not lower-fat)	75 mL
3 tbsp	curry powder	45 mL
1 lb	trimmed stewing beef, cut into 1-inch (2.5 cm) cubes	500 g
	Salt	
2 tbsp	oil (see Tips, left)	30 mL
1	bay leaf	1
1	cinnamon stick	1
3	whole cloves	3
4	green cardamom pods, crushed	4
1	large onion, halved and thinly sliced	1
3	cloves garlic, minced	3
2 tsp	minced gingerroot	10 mL
2 cups	beef broth	500 mL
¼ tsp	garam masala	1 mL

1. In a bowl, combine yogurt and curry powder and mix well. Add beef and toss to coat. Season to taste with salt. Cover and refrigerate for 24 hours.

2. In a large skillet or wok, heat oil over medium heat. Add bay leaf, cinnamon stick, cloves and cardamom pods and stir-fry for 1 minute, until fragrant. Add onion and stir-fry for 4 minutes, until softened. Add garlic and ginger and stir-fry for 1 minute. Add beef with marinade and stir-fry until well blended with seasonings.

3. Transfer to slow cooker stoneware and add beef broth. Cover and cook on Low for 8 hours or on High for 4 hours, until beef is meltingly tender. Taste and adjust seasoning. Stir in garam masala and serve immediately.

Curried Beef with Black-Eyed Peas

Serves 6

Tips

Serve this with plenty of hot rice to soak up the sauce.

For this quantity of black-eyed peas, cook ½ cup (125 mL) dried peas or use approximately half a can (14 to 19 oz/398 to 540 mL) of cooked black-eyed peas, drained and rinsed.

If you are using the outer stalks of celery, peel them first to get rid of the fibrous exterior.

Preparation Time: 15 minutes
Medium (approx. 4 quart) slow cooker
Heat Rating: 🌶🌶

2 tbsp	oil	30 mL
1¾ lbs	trimmed stewing beef, cut into 1-inch (2.5 cm) cubes and patted dry	875 g
1	onion, finely chopped	1
2 tbsp	curry powder	30 mL
1 tsp	dried thyme	5 mL
6	whole cloves	6
2	carrots, peeled and diced	2
2	stalks celery, diced (see Tips, left)	2
2	cloves garlic, minced	2
¼ cup	tomato paste	60 mL
2 cups	beef broth	500 mL
1	large potato, peeled and diced	1
1 cup	cooked black-eyed peas (see Tips, left)	250 mL
	Salt and freshly ground pepper	

1. In a skillet or wok, heat oil over medium-high heat. Add beef, in batches, and stir-fry until nicely browned, about 4 minutes a batch. Transfer to slow cooker stoneware as completed.

2. Lower heat to medium. Add onion, curry powder, thyme and cloves to pan and stir-fry until onion is softened, about 3 minutes. Add carrots, celery and garlic and stir-fry for 2 minutes. Stir in tomato paste. Add beef broth and stir-fry until blended with seasonings, scraping up brown bits from bottom of pan.

3. Transfer to slow cooker stoneware. Add potato and peas and stir well. Cover and cook on Low for 8 hours or on High for 4 hours, until beef is meltingly tender. Season to taste with salt and freshly ground pepper.

Burmese Beef & Potato Curry

Preparation Time: 15 minutes
Medium (approx. 4 quart) slow cooker
Heat Rating:

¼ cup	oil	60 mL
3 tbsp	medium curry paste	45 mL
2 tsp	ground coriander	10 mL
1 tsp	ground cumin	5 mL
1½ lbs	trimmed stewing beef, cut into 1-inch (2.5 cm) cubes and patted dry	750 g
	Salt and freshly ground black pepper	
2	potatoes, peeled and diced	2
2 cups	chicken broth	500 mL

1. In a large skillet or wok, heat oil over medium-high heat. Carefully add curry paste (it will splutter) and stir well. Reduce heat to low and cook for 10 minutes. If the mixture starts to burn, add a little water. When the paste is cooked, it should be golden brown and have a little oil around the edges.

2. Add coriander and cumin and stir-fry for 1 minute. Add beef and stir-fry until well coated with spice mixture. Season to taste with salt and freshly ground pepper.

3. Transfer to slow cooker stoneware. Add potatoes and broth. Cover and cook on Low for 8 hours or on High for 6 hours, until meat is meltingly tender. Serve immediately.

Thai-Style Red Curry with Beef

Tips

Serve with steamed jasmine rice.

Wild lime leaves, often called Kaffir lime leaves, are the leaves of a small Asian lime. You can use fresh or frozen varieties. If you can't find them for this recipe, substitute 1 tbsp (15 mL) finely grated lime zest.

To serve two people: Cut the quantities in half and use a small (approx. 2 quart) slow cooker.

To serve six people: Increase the quantities by half and use a large (approx. 5 quart) slow cooker.

Preparation Time: 20 minutes
Medium (approx. 4 quart) slow cooker
Heat Rating: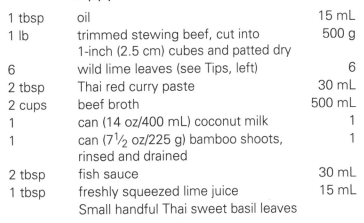

1 tbsp	oil	15 mL
1 lb	trimmed stewing beef, cut into 1-inch (2.5 cm) cubes and patted dry	500 g
6	wild lime leaves (see Tips, left)	6
2 tbsp	Thai red curry paste	30 mL
2 cups	beef broth	500 mL
1	can (14 oz/400 mL) coconut milk	1
1	can (7½ oz/225 g) bamboo shoots, rinsed and drained	1
2 tbsp	fish sauce	30 mL
1 tbsp	freshly squeezed lime juice	15 mL
	Small handful Thai sweet basil leaves	

1. In a skillet or wok, heat oil over medium-high heat. Add beef, in batches, and sauté until nicely browned, about 4 minutes a batch. Transfer to slow cooker stoneware as completed. Add lime leaves and curry paste to pan and sauté for 1 minute. Add broth and stir well. Pour over beef.

2. Cover and cook on Low for 8 hours or on High for 4 hours, until beef is meltingly tender. Increase heat to High, if necessary. Add coconut milk, drained bamboo shoots, fish sauce and lime juice and stir well. Cover and cook on High until bamboo shoots are heated through and flavors meld, about 15 minutes. Stir in basil just before serving.

Rangoon
Beef & Pumpkin Curry

Tips

Serve with an abundance of hot, fluffy rice.

To serve three people: Cut the quantities in half and use a small (approx. 2 quart) slow cooker.

To serve nine people: Increase the quantities by half and use a large (approx. 5 quart) slow cooker.

Variation

Substitute acorn or butternut squash for the pumpkin.

Preparation Time: 5 minutes
Medium (approx. 4 quart) slow cooker
Heat Rating:

¼ cup	oil	60 mL
¼ cup	mild curry paste	60 mL
1½ lbs	trimmed stewing beef, cut into 1-inch (2.5 cm) cubes and patted dry	750 g
5 cups	cubed (1 inch/2.5 cm) peeled pumpkin	1.25 mL
2 cups	water or beef broth	500 mL
	Salt and freshly ground black pepper	

1. In a large, deep frying pan, heat oil over medium-high heat. Carefully add curry paste (it will splutter) and stir well. Reduce heat to low and cook for 10 minutes. If the mixture starts to burn, add a little water. When the paste is cooked, it should be golden brown and have a little oil around the edges.

2. Add beef and pumpkin to the pan and stir-fry for 5 minutes. Add water and stir well, scraping up brown bits from bottom of pan.

3. Transfer to slow cooker stoneware. Cover and cook on Low for 8 hours or on High for 4 hours, until beef and pumpkin are tender. Season to taste with salt and freshly ground pepper.

Kofta Curry

Serves 6		

Tip

For a more mildly spiced result, reduce the quantity of cayenne to ½ tsp (2 mL).

Preparation time: 15 minutes
Medium (approx. 4 quart) slow cooker
Heat Rating: ♨♨

1½ lbs	lean ground beef	750 g
1 tbsp	minced gingerroot	15 mL
2	cloves garlic, minced	2
2 tsp	crushed fennel seeds	10 mL
1 tsp	ground cinnamon	5 mL
1 tsp	cayenne pepper (see Tips, left)	5 mL
	Salt and freshly ground black pepper	
2 cups	crushed tomatoes	500 mL
2 tbsp	curry powder	30 mL
1 tsp	ground turmeric	5 mL
1 tsp	granulated sugar	5 mL
½ cup	plain yogurt	125 mL
Pinch	cayenne pepper	Pinch
	Finely chopped mint leaves	

1. In a bowl, combine beef, ginger, garlic, fennel seeds, cinnamon and cayenne. Season to taste with salt and freshly ground black pepper. Mix well. Using your hands, form mixture into small, walnut-sized balls. Arrange in a single layer over bottom of slow cooker stoneware.

2. In a bowl, combine crushed tomatoes, curry powder, turmeric and sugar. Season to taste with salt and freshly ground pepper.

3. Pour tomato mixture over meatballs. Cover and cook on Low for 6 to 8 hours or on High for 3 to 4 hours, until meatballs are cooked through. Drizzle with yogurt, sprinkle with cayenne and garnish with mint. Serve immediately.

Kheema Mutter

Serves 4

Tips

Serve with warm naan.

If you can't find curry leaves, substitute dried or fresh bay leaves.

Variation

Substitute ground lamb for the beef.

Preparation time: 15 minutes
Medium (approx. 4 quart) slow cooker
Heat Rating: ◊◊

1 lb	lean ground beef	500 mL
2 tbsp	medium curry paste	30 mL
3	cloves garlic, minced	3
2 tsp	minced gingerroot	10 mL
¼ tsp	ground turmeric	1 mL
2 tbsp	oil	30 mL
1	large onion, finely chopped	1
10	curry leaves	10
2	long green chile peppers, minced	2
6	ripe tomatoes, coarsely chopped	6
1 cup	coconut milk	250 mL
¼ cup	finely chopped cilantro leaves	60 mL
1 cup	green peas, thawed if frozen	250 mL

1. In a bowl, combine beef, curry paste, garlic, ginger and turmeric. Mix well and set aside.

2. In a skillet or wok, heat oil over medium heat. Add onion, curry leaves and chiles and stir-fry until onions are softened, about 3 minutes. Increase heat to high. Add beef mixture and stir-fry for 3 minutes. Stir in tomatoes and scrape up brown bits from bottom of pan.

3. Transfer to slow cooker stoneware and add coconut milk. Cover and cook on Low for 3 to 4 hours or on High for 1½ to 2 hours. Add cilantro and peas and stir well. Cover and cook on High for 15 minutes, until peas are tender.

Curried Oxtail

Tips

Serve this with an abundance of hot rice.

Because there is so much bone in oxtails, you will need to use a large (approximately 5 quart) slow cooker to make this recipe.

For this quantity of lima beans, cook 1 cup (250 mL) dried lima beans, or use 1 can (14 to 19 oz/398 to 540 mL) cooked lima beans, drained and rinsed. You can also use 2 cups (500 mL) frozen lima beans, thawed.

Preparation Time: 30 minutes
Large (approx. 5 quart) slow cooker
Heat Rating: ♨♨

3 lbs	oxtails, cut into 2-inch (5 cm) pieces	1. 5 kg
	Salt and freshly ground black pepper	
2 tbsp	oil	30 mL
2	onions, finely chopped	2
4	carrots, peeled and thinly sliced	4
3	cloves garlic, finely chopped	3
1	long red chile pepper, seeded and minced	1
2 tsp	curry powder	10 mL
1 tsp	dried thyme	5 mL
½ tsp	ground cinnamon	2 mL
½ tsp	ground coriander	2 mL
½ tsp	ground allspice	2 mL
½ tsp	ground nutmeg	2 mL
1	can (14 oz/398 mL) diced tomatoes, with juice	1
2 cups	beef broth	500 mL
2 cups	cooked lima beans (see Tips, left)	500 mL

1. Bring a large pot of water to a boil. Add oxtails and return to a boil. Reduce heat and simmer for 10 minutes. Using a slotted spoon, transfer to a plate lined with paper towels to drain. Pat dry and season to taste with salt and freshly ground black pepper.

2. In a large skillet or wok, heat oil over medium-high heat. Add oxtails, in batches, and sauté until nicely browned, about 6 minutes a batch. Transfer to stoneware as completed. When all the oxtails have been browned, lower heat to medium.

3. Add onions and carrots to pan and stir-fry until softened, about 5 minutes. Add garlic, chile pepper, curry powder, thyme, cinnamon, coriander, allspice and nutmeg and stir-fry for 1 minute. Add tomatoes with juice and bring to a boil, stirring and scraping up brown bits from bottom of pan.

4. Transfer to slow cooker stoneware. Stir in beef broth and lima beans. Cover and cook on Low for 8 hours or on High for 4 hours, until oxtails are meltingly tender.

Vietnamese Spiced Beef & Noodle Broth

Serves 4

Tips

To serve two people: Cut the quantities in half and use a small (approx. 2 quart) slow cooker.

To serve six people: Increase the quantities by half and use a large (approx. 5 quart) slow cooker.

Preparation time: 20 minutes, plus soaking
Medium (approx. 4 quart) slow cooker
4 large serving bowls
Heat rating: ♨♨

Broth

4 cups	beef broth	1 L
6	whole cloves	6
10	whole black peppercorns	10
1	piece (2 inches/5 cm) peeled gingerroot, thinly sliced	1
3	cinnamon sticks	3
3	star anise	3
6	green cardamom pods	6

Pho

5 oz	dried rice noodles	150 g
2 tbsp	fish sauce	30 mL
8 oz	beef sirloin or tenderloin, thinly sliced	250 g

Garnishes

¼ cup	mint leaves	60 mL
¼ cup	chopped cilantro leaves	60 mL
6	green onions, white and green parts, finely sliced	6
2 oz	bean sprouts	60 g
1	long red chile pepper, thinly sliced	1
2	limes, cut into wedges	2

1. *Broth:* In slow cooker stoneware, combine beef broth, cloves, peppercorns, ginger, cinnamon, star anise and cardamom. Cover and cook on Low for 6 hours or on High for 3 hours, periodically skimming off impurities that float to the top. Place a fine-mesh strainer over a large saucepan and strain. Discard solids and return broth to stoneware.

2. *Pho:* Stir in noodles and fish sauce. Cover and cook on Low until noodles are softened, about 20 minutes.

3. To serve, divide beef equally among warmed serving bowls. Ladle the hot broth and noodles over each bowl, dividing equally. Serve immediately, passing the garnishes at the table.

Cambodian Pork & Lemongrass Curry

Tips

Serve with fluffy rice.

Before chopping the lemongrass, be sure to remove the tough outer leaves.

Many butchers sell cut-up pork stewing meat, which is fine to use in this recipe.

Be sure to use tamarind paste (sometimes labeled "concentrate"), which comes in a jar. Tamarind in a block needs to be dissolved in water and pressed through a sieve to remove seeds and pulp before being added to recipes and, therefore, becomes more diluted in flavor and texture.

Preparation Time: 20 minutes
Medium (approx. 4 quart) slow cooker
Heat Rating: 🌶🌶

2 tbsp	oil	30 mL
6	shallots, finely chopped	6
2 tbsp	finely chopped lemongrass (see Tips, left)	30 mL
1 tbsp	minced gingerroot	15 mL
1 tbsp	minced garlic	15 mL
1 tbsp	ground cumin	15 mL
2 tsp	crushed fenugreek seeds	10 mL
1 tsp	ground turmeric	5 mL
1¼ lbs	trimmed pork shoulder or blade (butt), cut into 1-inch (2.5 cm) cubes and patted dry (see Tips, left)	625 g
	Salt and freshly ground black pepper	
1 tbsp	tamarind paste (see Tips, left)	15 mL
1 tsp	finely grated lime zest	5 mL
2 tbsp	freshly squeezed lime juice	30 mL
1	can (14 oz/400 mL) coconut milk	1
8	baby new potatoes, quartered	8
2	red bell peppers, seeded and chopped	2
1	long red chile pepper, thinly sliced	1

1. In a large skillet or wok, heat oil over medium-high heat. Add shallots, lemongrass, gingerroot, garlic, cumin, fenugreek and turmeric and sauté until softened, about 3 minutes. Add pork and sauté until lightly browned, about 4 minutes. Season to taste with salt and freshly ground black pepper.

2. Transfer to slow cooker stoneware. Stir in tamarind paste, lime zest and juice, coconut milk and potatoes. Cover and cook on Low for 3 to 4 hours or on High for 1½ to 2 hours, until potatoes are cooked and pork is meltingly tender. Stir in bell peppers and chile pepper. Cover and cook on High for 15 minutes, until peppers are tender. Ladle into warm bowls.

Pork Rendang

Serves 6

Tips

Serve with steamed jasmine rice.

Before chopping the lemongrass, be sure to remove the tough outer leaves.

Many butchers sell cut-up pork stewing meat, which is fine to use in this recipe.

If you prefer a milder curry, reduce the number of chile peppers to suit your taste.

To serve three people: Cut the quantities in half and use a small (approx. 2 quart) slow cooker.

To serve nine people: Increase the quantities by half and use a large (approx. 5 quart) slow cooker.

Preparation Time: 15 minutes
Medium (approx. 4 quart) slow cooker
Heat Rating: 🌶🌶🌶

2	onions, chopped	2
1/3 cup	finely chopped lemongrass (see Tips, left)	75 mL
1/4 cup	finely chopped cilantro (leaves and stems)	60 mL
6	cloves garlic, chopped	6
3	Thai bird's-eye chile peppers, chopped (see Tips, left)	3
1 tbsp	ground coriander	15 mL
1 tsp	ground turmeric	5 mL
1	can (14 oz/400 mL) coconut milk	1
2 tbsp	oil	30 mL
2 lbs	trimmed pork shoulder or blade (butt), cut into 1-inch (2.5 cm) cubes and patted dry (see Tips, left)	500 g
	Salt and freshly ground black pepper	

1. In a food processor fitted with the metal blade, pulse onions, lemongrass, cilantro, garlic, chiles, coriander and turmeric until finely chopped and blended. Add coconut milk and process until smooth and blended. Set aside.

2. In a large skillet or wok, heat oil over medium-high heat. Add pork, in batches, and sauté until browned, about 4 minutes a batch. Transfer to slow cooker stoneware as completed.

3. Add onion mixture to stoneware. Season to taste with salt and freshly ground pepper. Cover and cook on Low for 8 hours or on High for 4 hours, until pork is meltingly tender.

Pork Vindaloo

Tips

Many butchers sell cut-up pork stewing meat, which is fine to use in this recipe.

Vindaloo curry paste is available in Asian markets or the Asian section of well-stocked supermarkets. Some are mild and others are quite hot, so taste yours and adjust the quantity of cayenne accordingly.

The quantity of cayenne you use will depend on how spicy your curry paste is. You may want to increase or decrease it accordingly.

Preparation Time: 15 minutes, plus marinating
Medium (approx. 4 quart) slow cooker
Heat rating: ♨♨♨

1¼ lbs	trimmed pork shoulder or blade (butt), cut into 1-inch (2.5 cm) cubes and patted dry (see Tips, left)	625 g
¼ cup	vindaloo curry paste (see Tips, left)	60 mL
2 tbsp	oil	30 mL
1	onion, finely chopped	1
1 tsp	cayenne pepper (see Tips, left)	5 mL
2 tsp	ground cumin	10 mL
1 tsp	ground turmeric	5 mL
⅓ cup	tomato paste	75 mL
1 tbsp	granulated sugar	15 mL
1	can (14 oz/398 mL) diced tomatoes, with juice	1
4	potatoes, peeled and diced	4
2 cups	chicken broth	500 mL
	Salt and freshly ground black pepper	
	Chopped cilantro leaves	

1. Place pork in a bowl. Rub the curry paste all over the meat so it is well mixed in. Cover and refrigerate for at least 6 hours or up to 24 hours.

2. In a large skillet or wok, heat oil over medium-high heat. Add onion and stir-fry until softened, about 3 minutes. Add cayenne, cumin, turmeric and reserved pork and stir-fry for 4 minutes. Stir in tomato paste and sugar. Add tomatoes with juice and bring to a boil, scraping up brown bits on bottom of pan.

3. Transfer to slow cooker stoneware. Add potatoes and broth and stir well. Cover and cook on Low for 8 hours or on High for 4 hours, until pork is meltingly tender.

Bangkok-Style Sour Curry with Pork

Serves 6

Tips

Serve this accompanied by thick egg noodles.

This produces a very hot result. If you're heat-averse, reduce the quantity of curry paste to suit your taste, for example, to 1 or 2 tbsp (15 to 30 mL).

Many butchers sell cut-up pork stewing meat, which is fine to use in this recipe.

Be sure to use tamarind paste (sometimes labeled "concentrate"), which comes in a jar. Tamarind in a block needs to be dissolved in water and pressed through a sieve to remove seeds and pulp before being added to recipes and, therefore, becomes more diluted in flavor and texture.

Wild lime leaves, often called Kaffir lime leaves, are the leaves of a small Asian lime. You can use fresh or frozen varieties. If you can't find them for this recipe, substitute 1 tbsp (15 mL) finely grated lime zest.

Palm sugar is also known as jaggery. You can substitute raw cane sugar, such as Mexican piloncillo, or regular dark brown sugar.

Preparation Time: 20 minutes
Medium (approx. 4 quart) slow cooker
Heat Rating: 🌶🌶🌶

1 tbsp	oil	15 mL
1	onion, finely chopped	1
2 tsp	minced gingerroot	10 mL
3 tbsp	Thai red curry paste (see Tips, left)	45 mL
1¾ lbs	trimmed pork shoulder or blade (butt), cut into 1-inch (2.5 cm) cubes and patted dry (see Tips, left)	875 g
2 cups	chicken broth	500 mL
¼ cup	finely chopped cilantro, leaves and stems	60 mL
2	stalks lemongrass, crushed	2
¼ cup	tamarind paste (see Tips, left)	60 mL
1 tbsp	soft palm sugar (see Tips, left)	15 mL
6	wild lime leaves (see Tips, left)	6
	Small handful Thai sweet basil leaves	

1. In a large skillet or wok, heat oil over medium heat. Add onion and stir-fry until softened, about 3 minutes. Add ginger, red curry paste and pork and stir-fry until meat is well-coated with mixture, about 5 minutes. Add broth and stir well, scraping up brown bits from bottom of pan.

2. Transfer to slow cooker stoneware. Add cilantro, lemongrass, tamarind paste, sugar and lime leaves. Cover and cook on Low for 8 hours, until pork is meltingly tender. Add basil and serve immediately.

Burmese Red Curry with Pork

Tips

Many butchers sell cut-up pork stewing meat, which is fine to use in this recipe.

To serve three people: Cut the quantities in half and use a small (approx. 2 quart) slow cooker.

To serve nine people: Increase the quantities by half and use a large (approx. 5 quart) slow cooker.

Preparation Time: 10 minutes, plus marinating
Medium (approx. 4 quart) slow cooker
Heat rating:

½ cup	soy sauce	125 mL
½ cup	tomato paste	125 mL
1¾ lbs	trimmed pork shoulder or blade (butt), cut into 1-inch (2.5 cm) cubes and patted dry (see Tips, left)	875 g
2 tbsp	oil	30 mL
1 tbsp	brown sugar	15 mL
1 tbsp	curry powder	15 mL
2	cloves garlic, minced	2
1 tbsp	minced gingerroot	15 mL

1. In a small bowl, combine soy sauce and tomato paste. Place pork in a non-reactive dish and add the soy mixture. Toss to coat evenly. Cover and refrigerate for at least 6 hours or overnight.

2. In a large skillet or wok, heat oil over medium heat. Add sugar and cook, stirring, until sugar is dissolved and just starting to caramelize. Add curry powder, garlic and ginger and cook, stirring, for 2 minutes. Add pork, with marinade, and stir until well combined.

3. Transfer to slow cooker stoneware. Add just enough water to cover. Cover and cook on Low for 8 hours or on High for 4 hours, until pork is meltingly tender.

Ceylonese Black Curry with Pork

Tips

Be sure to use tamarind paste (sometimes labeled "concentrate"), which comes in a jar. Tamarind in a block needs to be dissolved in water and pressed through a sieve to remove seeds and pulp before being added to recipes and, therefore, becomes more diluted in flavor and texture.

If you can't find curry leaves, substitute dried or fresh bay leaves.

Many butchers sell cut-up pork stewing meat, which is fine to use in this recipe.

Coconut cream is thicker and richer than coconut milk. You can simply skim off the top half of a can of coconut milk (be sure not to shake it before opening). Or, if you are using coconut powder, follow the instructions but substitute heavy or whipping (35%) cream for the water.

To serve three people: Cut the quantities in half and use a small (approx. 2 quart) slow cooker.

To serve nine people: Increase the quantities by half and use a large (approx. 5 quart) slow cooker.

Preparation Time: 15 minutes
Medium (approx. 4 quart) slow cooker
Heat Rating: ◊◊

¾ cup	water	175 mL
1 tbsp	tamarind paste (see Tips, left)	15 mL
2	onions, coarsely chopped	2
2 tbsp	coarsely chopped gingerroot	30 mL
4	cloves garlic, coarsely chopped	4
2 tbsp	oil	30 mL
6	curry leaves (see Tips, left)	6
1	piece (2 inches/5 cm) cinnamon stick	1
8	cardamom pods	8
2 tbsp	curry powder	30 mL
1¾ lbs	trimmed pork shoulder or blade (butt), cut into 1-inch (2.5 cm) cubes and patted dry (see Tips, left)	875 g
1 tbsp	white wine vinegar	15 mL
¾ cup	coconut cream (see Tips, left)	175 mL
1	long red chile pepper, finely sliced	1

1. In a small bowl, whisk together water and tamarind paste. Set aside.

2. In a food processor fitted with the metal blade, process onions, ginger and garlic until finely chopped.

3. In a skillet or wok, heat oil over medium heat. Add onion mixture and stir-fry until softened, about 3 minutes. Add curry leaves, cinnamon stick, cardamom and curry powder and stir-fry for 1 minute, until fragrant. Add pork and stir-fry until well coated with mixture, about 2 minutes. Stir in reserved tamarind water and vinegar.

4. Transfer to slow cooker stoneware. Cover and cook on Low for 8 hours or on High for 4 hours, until pork is meltingly tender. Stir in coconut cream and chile pepper and serve immediately.

Indonesian Pork Curry

Tips

Many butchers sell cut-up pork stewing meat, which is fine to use in this recipe.

To purée garlic and gingerroot, use a fine, sharp-toothed grater, such as those made by Microplane.

Preparation Time: 20 minutes
Medium (approx. 4 quart) slow cooker
Heat Rating: ♨♨

2 tbsp	oil	30 mL
1¾ lbs	trimmed boneless pork shoulder or blade (butt), cut into bite-size pieces	1 kg
1	onion, finely chopped	1
10	curry leaves	10
2 tsp	puréed garlic (see Tips, left)	10 mL
2 tsp	puréed gingerroot (see Tips, left)	10 mL
1 tbsp	cumin seeds	15 mL
1 tbsp	crushed coriander seeds	15 mL
2 tbsp	medium curry powder	30 mL
1 cup	water	250 mL
2 tbsp	white wine vinegar	30 mL
1	can (14 oz/400 mL) coconut milk	1
2	pieces (each 2 inches/5 cm) cinnamon stick	2
2	star anise	2
6	green cardamom pods, bruised	6
	Salt and freshly ground black pepper	

1. In a skillet or wok, heat oil over medium-high heat. Add pork, in batches if necessary, and stir-fry until browned, about 4 minutes a batch. Using a slotted spoon, transfer to slow cooker stoneware as completed.

2. Add onion, curry leaves, garlic, ginger and cumin and coriander seeds to pan and stir-fry for 4 minutes. Add curry powder and stir-fry until fragrant, about 2 minutes. Add water and vinegar and stir, scraping up brown bits from bottom of pan.

3. Transfer onion mixture to slow cooker stoneware. Add coconut milk, cinnamon, star anise and cardamom and stir well. Season to taste with salt and freshly ground pepper. Cover and cook on Low for 6 hours or on High for 3 hours, until pork is very tender. Serve immediately.

Spiced Braised Pork

Tips

This dish is delicious served with steamed greens and plenty of rice.

For best results, use a raw cane sugar such as dark muscovado or succanat.

To purée gingerroot, use a fine, sharp-toothed grater, such as those made by Microplane.

Adjust the quantity of cayenne pepper to suit your taste.

Preparation time: 10 minutes
Medium (approx. 4 quart) slow cooker
Heat Rating: ◑

1¾ lbs	trimmed boneless pork shoulder or blade (butt), sliced into 12 pieces	1 kg
	Salt	
1 tbsp	dark brown sugar (see Tips, left)	15 mL
1 tbsp	puréed gingerroot (see Tips, left)	15 mL
2	cloves garlic, sliced	2
2 tsp	cayenne pepper (see Tips, left)	10 mL
3	pieces (each 2 inches/5 cm) cinnamon stick	3
3	cloves	3
10	black peppercorns	10
3	star anise	3
2 cups	good-quality beef broth	500 mL
½ cup	soy sauce	125 mL
	Finely grated zest and juice of 1 large orange	

1. Place sliced pork in a large, heavy saucepan and add water to cover. Bring to a boil over high heat. Cover, reduce heat and simmer gently for 30 minutes. Drain well.

2. Arrange pork slices evenly over bottom of slow cooker stoneware. Season to taste with salt. Add brown sugar, ginger, garlic, cayenne, cinnamon, cloves, peppercorns and star anise scattering seasonings evenly over pork. Add beef broth, soy sauce and orange zest and juice. Cover and cook on Low for 6 hours, until pork is meltingly tender. Serve immediately.

Nonya Pork Curry

Serves 6

Tips

Serve this dish with plenty of hot steamed rice.

Nonya is a type of cuisine that incorporates various Southeast Asian influences such as Indonesian and Malaysian.

Ketcap asin is a salty Indonesian soy sauce that is available in Asian markets. If you can't find it, substitute 1 tbsp (15 mL) dark soy sauce mixed with 1 tsp (5 mL) fish sauce such as nam pla.

Preparation Time: 25 minutes, plus chilling
Medium (approx. 4 quart) slow cooker
Heat Rating: ◊◊◊

Meatballs

1¾ lbs	ground pork	875 g
1	egg	1
2 tbsp	finely chopped cilantro leaves	30 mL
2	long red or bird's-eye chile peppers, minced	2
2	cloves garlic, minced	2
2 tsp	cornstarch	10 mL
	Salt and freshly ground black pepper	

Curry Sauce

½ cup	chopped shallots	125 mL
2 tbsp	oil	30 mL
6	long red or bird's-eye chile peppers, coarsely chopped	6
4	cloves garlic, chopped	4
1 tbsp	coarsely chopped gingerroot	15 mL
1	can (14 oz/398 mL) diced tomatoes, with juice	1
1 tbsp	kecap asin (see Tips, left)	15 mL
1	can (14 oz/400 mL) coconut milk	1

1. *Meatballs:* In a bowl, combine pork, egg, cilantro, chiles, garlic and cornstarch. Season to taste with salt and freshly ground pepper. Mix well and shape into walnut-sized balls. Place on a baking sheet, cover and refrigerate for at least 3 hours or overnight.

2. *Curry Sauce:* In a food processor fitted with the metal blade, process shallots, oil, chiles, garlic and ginger into a fine paste. Add tomatoes, kecap asin and coconut milk and pulse to blend.

3. Arrange meatballs over bottom of slow cooker stoneware and add curry sauce. Cover and cook on High for 4 hours, until sauce is hot and bubbly and meatballs are cooked through.

Filipino Minced Meat Curry

Tips

Serve over steamed rice or egg noodles.

Be sure to shake the can of coconut milk well before using, as the cream layer collects on the top after it's been sitting.

Variation

Substitute an equal quantity of ground chicken for the pork.

Preparation Time: 10 minutes
Medium (approx. 4 quart) slow cooker
Heat Rating:

2 tbsp	oil	30 mL
1½ lbs	ground pork	750 g
3	cloves garlic, minced	3
1 tbsp	minced gingerroot	15 mL
2 tbsp	curry powder	30 mL
1 tsp	ground turmeric	5 mL
2	long green chile peppers, minced	2
1	can (14 oz/400 mL) coconut milk	1
2	bay leaves	2
	Salt and freshly ground black pepper	
1 cup	green peas, thawed if frozen	250 mL
2 tbsp	freshly squeezed lime juice	30 mL

1. In a large skillet or wok, heat oil over medium-high heat. Add pork and stir-fry until browned, about 4 minutes. Using a slotted spoon, transfer to slow cooker stoneware.

2. Add garlic, ginger, curry powder, turmeric and chiles to pan and stir-fry until fragrant, about 2 minutes. Add to stoneware and stir well. Add coconut milk and bay leaves. Season to taste with salt and freshly ground black pepper. Stir well. Cover and cook on Low for 4 hours or on High for 2 hours. Stir in peas. Cover and cook on High for 15 minutes, until peas are tender. Stir in lime juice and serve.

Burmese Lamb Curry

Tips

If you prefer a spicier result, use an equal quantity of hot curry paste.

To serve two people: Cut the quantities in half and use a small (approx. 2 quart) slow cooker.

To serve six people: Increase the quantities by half and use a large (approx. 5 quart) slow cooker.

Preparation Time: 10 minutes
Medium (approx. 4 quart) slow cooker
Heat Rating: ♨

2 tbsp	oil	30 mL
1 lb	trimmed stewing lamb, cut into 1-inch (2.5 cm) pieces and patted dry	500 g
1	can (14 oz/398 mL) diced tomatoes, with juice	1
2 tbsp	mild curry paste (see Tips, left)	30 mL
2 tsp	ground turmeric	10 mL
10 oz	new potatoes, quartered	300 g
	Chopped cilantro leaves	

1. In a skillet or wok, heat oil over medium-high heat. Add lamb, in batches, and stir-fry until browned, about 4 minutes a batch. Transfer to slow cooker stoneware as completed. Add tomatoes with juice, curry paste and turmeric to pan and stir well, scraping up brown bits from bottom of pan.

2. Transfer to slow cooker stoneware and add potatoes and water just to cover. Cover and cook on Low for 8 hours or on High for 4 hours, until lamb is very tender. Garnish with cilantro just before serving.

Kashmiri Almond Saffron & Lamb Curry

Serves 6

Tips

You can adjust the heat level of this curry by increasing or decreasing the quantity of dried red chile peppers.

To serve three people: Cut the quantities in half and use a small (approx. 2 quart) slow cooker.

To serve nine people: Increase the quantities by half and use a large (approx. 5 quart) slow cooker.

Preparation Time: 30 minutes
Medium (approx. 4 quart) slow cooker
Heat Rating: 🌶🌶

1 tbsp	saffron threads	15 mL
1½ cups	warm water	375 mL
2 tbsp	oil	30 mL
3	onions, thinly sliced	3
2	cloves garlic, minced	2
2 tsp	minced gingerroot	10 mL
3	dried red chile peppers (see Tips, left)	3
8	green cardamom pods	8
2 tsp	ground cumin	10 mL
1 tsp	ground coriander	5 mL
1 tsp	garam masala	5 mL
1 tsp	fennel seeds	5 mL
½ tsp	ground turmeric	2 mL
2 lb	trimmed stewing lamb, cut into 1-inch (2.5 cm) pieces and patted dry	1 kg
	Salt and freshly ground black pepper	
½ cup	toasted blanched almonds	125 mL
½ cup	heavy or whipping (35%) cream	125 mL
⅓ cup	plain yogurt (not lower-fat)	75 mL

1. In a bowl, combine saffron and water. Set aside for 15 minutes to infuse.

2. Meanwhile, in a large skillet or wok, heat oil over medium heat. Add onions, garlic, ginger and chiles and stir-fry until onions are softened, about 3 minutes. Add cardamom, cumin, coriander, garam masala, fennel seeds and turmeric and stir-fry until fragrant, about 2 minutes. Increase heat to medium-high. Add lamb and stir-fry until browned, about 6 minutes. Stir in saffron water, scraping up brown bits from bottom of pan.

3. Transfer to slow cooker stoneware. Season to taste with salt and freshly ground black pepper. Cover and cook on Low for 8 hours or on High for 4 hours, until lamb is meltingly tender. Add almonds, cream and yogurt and stir well. Cover and cook on High for 15 minutes to meld flavors.

Creamy Lamb Korma

Tips

Serve this with warm naan or parathas.

Korma paste is available in Asian markets or the Asian section of well-stocked supermarkets.

White poppy seeds are traditionally used in Indian cooking. If you can't find them, substitute black poppy seeds or sesame seeds.

To serve three people: Cut the quantities in half and use a small (approx. 2 quart) slow cooker.

To serve nine people: Increase the quantities by half and use a large (approx. 5 quart) slow cooker.

Preparation Time: 15 minutes
Medium (approx. 4 quart) slow cooker
Heat rating:

2 tbsp	oil	30 mL
1¾ lbs	trimmed stewing lamb, cut into 1-inch (2.5 cm) cubes and patted dry	875 g
1	onion, finely chopped	1
1 tbsp	minced gingerroot	15 mL
2	cloves garlic, minced	2
⅓ cup	ground almonds	75 mL
1 tbsp	white poppy seeds (see Tips, left)	15 mL
⅓ cup	korma paste (see Tips, left)	75 mL
1½ cups	chicken or lamb broth	375 mL
	Salt and freshly ground black pepper	
1 cup	table (10%) cream	250 mL

1. In a large skillet or wok, heat oil over medium-high heat. Add lamb, in batches, and stir-fry until browned, about 4 minutes a batch. Using a slotted spoon, transfer to slow cooker stoneware as completed.

2. Lower heat to medium. Add onion, ginger and garlic to pan and cook, stirring, until onion is softened, about 3 minutes. Add ground almonds, poppy seeds and korma paste and cook, stirring, for about 2 minutes. Stir in chicken broth, scraping up brown bits from bottom of pan. Season to taste with salt and freshly ground pepper.

3. Transfer to slow cooker stoneware and stir well. Cover and cook on Low for 8 hours or on High for 4 hours, until lamb is very tender. Stir in cream. Cover and cook on High for 10 minutes, until heated through.

Lamb Rogan Josh

Tips

Make an effort to get Kashmiri chile powder, which is milder than most Indian chile powders. Along with the paprika, it will help to ensure that the dish is a vibrant red color, which is essential to dishes described as rogan josh. If you can't find it, cayenne will produce an acceptable result in terms of the flavor.

Be sure to cut your potatoes into small pieces, about ¼ inch (0.5 cm). Otherwise they won't be cooked when the lamb is done.

Preparation Time: 20 minutes
Medium (approx. 4 quart) slow cooker
Heat Rating: ♨♨

2 tbsp	oil	30 mL
1¼ lbs	trimmed stewing lamb, cut into 1-inch (2.5 cm) cubes and patted dry	625 g
2	large onions, halved and sliced	2
3	cloves garlic, minced	3
1 tbsp	minced gingerroot	15 mL
2	pieces (each 2 inches/5 cm) cinnamon stick	2
2 tsp	sweet paprika	10 mL
2 tsp	Kashmiri chile powder or 1 tsp (5 mL) cayenne pepper (see Tips, left)	10 mL
6	green cardamom pods, crushed	6
¼ cup	curry paste	60 mL
6 tbsp	tomato paste	90 mL
1	can (14 oz/398 mL) diced tomatoes, with juice	1
1 tsp	granulated sugar	5 mL
2 cups	chicken or lamb broth	500 mL
4	potatoes, peeled and diced (see Tips, left)	4
	Salt and freshly ground black pepper	
	Finely chopped cilantro leaves	

1. In a large skillet or wok, heat oil over medium-high heat. Add lamb, in batches, and stir-fry until nicely browned, about 4 minutes a batch. Transfer to slow cooker stoneware as completed.

2. Lower heat to medium. Add onions and stir-fry until softened and lightly browned, about 10 minutes. Add garlic, ginger, cinnamon, paprika, chile powder and cardamom pods. Stir-fry until nicely fragrant, about 2 minutes. Stir in curry paste. Add tomato paste, tomatoes with juice and sugar. Stir well, scraping up brown bits from bottom of pan.

Tips

To serve two people: Cut the quantities in half and use a small (approx. 2 quart) slow cooker.

To serve six people: Increase the quantities by half and use a large (approx. 5 quart) slow cooker.

3. Transfer to slow cooker stoneware. Add broth and potatoes and stir well. Season to taste with salt and freshly ground pepper. Cover and cook on Low for 8 hours or on High for 4 hours, until lamb is meltingly tender. Garnish with cilantro before serving.

Fragrant Lamb Curry

Serves 4

Tips

Serve with fluffy basmati rice.

To serve two people: Cut the quantities in half and use a small (approx. 2 quart) slow cooker.

To serve six people: Increase the quantities by half and use a large (approx. 5 quart) slow cooker.

Preparation Time: 15 minutes
Medium (approx. 4 quart) slow cooker
Heat Rating: ♨♨♨

2 tbsp	oil	30 mL
1¼ lbs	trimmed stewing lamb, cut into 1-inch (2.5 cm) cubes and patted dry	625 g
2	onions, finely chopped	2
1 tbsp	minced gingerroot	15 mL
1	long red chile pepper, minced	1
1 tbsp	ground cumin	15 mL
½ tsp	ground cinnamon	2 mL
½ tsp	ground coriander	2 mL
½ tsp	ground allspice	2 mL
½ tsp	ground nutmeg	2 mL
1	can (14 oz/398 mL) diced tomatoes, with juice	1
⅓ cup	light brown sugar	75 g
	Salt and freshly ground black pepper	
1	red bell pepper, seeded and chopped	1
1 tbsp	finely grated lime zest	15 mL
¼ cup	freshly squeezed lime juice	60 mL

1. In a skillet or wok, heat oil over medium-high heat. Add lamb, in batches, and stir-fry until browned, about 4 minutes a batch. Using a slotted spoon, transfer to slow cooker stoneware as completed.

2. Lower heat to medium. Add onions to pan and stir-fry until softened, about 3 minutes. Add ginger, chile, cumin, cinnamon, coriander, allspice and nutmeg and cook, stirring, for 1 minute. Stir in tomatoes and sugar, scraping up brown bits from bottom of pan. Season to taste with salt and freshly ground pepper.

3. Transfer to slow cooker stoneware. Cover and cook on Low for 8 hours or on High for 4 hours, until lamb is meltingly tender. Stir in red pepper, lime zest and lime juice. Cover and cook on High for 15 minutes, until pepper is tender. Serve immediately.

Massaman Lamb Curry

Serves 6

Tips

Serve with steamed jasmine or Thai rice.

Massaman curry paste is available in well-stocked Asian markets or online.

Be sure to use tamarind paste (sometimes labeled "concentrate"), which comes in a jar. Tamarind in a block needs to be dissolved in water and pressed through a sieve to remove seeds and pulp before being added to recipes and, therefore, becomes more diluted in flavor and texture.

Remove the tough outer layers of the lemongrass and cut the remaining stalk into several sections. Using the flat side of the knife, smash each piece. This helps to release the flavor.

Preparation Time: 15 minutes
Medium (approx. 4 quart) slow cooker
Heat Rating: ♨♨

1¾ lbs	trimmed stewing lamb, cut into 1-inch (2.5 cm) cubes	875 g
1½ cups	diced butternut squash	375 mL
16	shallots, peeled but left whole	16
3 tbsp	massaman curry paste (see Tips, left)	45 mL
2 tbsp	tamarind paste (see Tips, left)	30 mL
2	stalks lemongrass, smashed (see Tips, left)	2
3 cups	coconut milk	750 mL
2 cups	lamb broth	500 mL
	Finely chopped green onions	

1. In slow cooker stoneware, combine lamb, squash, shallots, curry paste, tamarind paste, lemongrass, coconut milk and broth. Stir well.

2. Cover and cook on Low for 8 hours or on High for 3 hours, until lamb is very tender. Serve immediately, garnished with green onions.

Sri Lankan Lamb Curry

Tips

Sri Lankan curry powder usually contains sweeter spices, such as cardamom and cinnamon, as well as curry leaves. Because the spices are roasted before being ground, the flavor tends to be deeper than that of Indian curry powder. Look for it in well-stocked Asian markets or purchase online.

If you can't find curry leaves, substitute dried or fresh bay leaves.

Preparation Time: 10 minutes, plus marinating
Medium (approx. 4 quart) slow cooker
Heat Rating: ♨♨

1¾ lbs	trimmed stewing lamb, cut into bite-size pieces	875 g
¼ cup	white wine vinegar	60 mL
2	onions, quartered	2
5	cloves garlic	5
3 tbsp	coarsely chopped gingerroot	45 mL
2 tbsp	oil	30 mL
¼ cup	Sri Lankan curry powder (see Tips, left)	60 mL
12	curry leaves (see Tips, left)	12
2 cups	coconut milk	500 mL

1. Place lamb in a bowl. Add vinegar, stir well and set aside to marinate for 30 minutes. When you're ready to cook, drain lamb, reserving liquid. Pat meat dry and set lamb and liquid aside.

2. Meanwhile, in a food processor fitted with the metal blade, process onions, garlic and ginger to a smooth paste, adding a bit of water if necessary.

3. In a large skillet or wok, heat oil over medium heat. Add onion paste and stir-fry for 3 minutes. Add curry powder and curry leaves and stir-fry for 3 minutes. Add drained lamb and stir-fry until it begins to brown, about 5 minutes. Add reserved marinating liquid and bring to a boil, scraping up brown bits from bottom of pan.

4. Transfer to slow cooker stoneware and add coconut milk. Cover and cook on Low for 6 hours, until lamb is tender. Serve immediately.

Spicy Lamb Shanks

Serves 4 to 8

Tips

Whether you cook the lamb shanks whole or have them cut into halves or pieces is a matter of preference. However, if the shanks are left whole, you will be able to serve only four people — each will receive one large shank.

Because there is so much bone in lamb shanks, you will need to use a large (approx. 5 quart) slow cooker for this recipe.

Preparation Time: 20 minutes
Large (approx. 5 quart) slow cooker
Heat Rating: 🔥

2 tbsp	oil	30 mL
4	large lamb shanks (about 4 lbs/2 kg) (see Tips, left)	4
2 tsp	ground cinnamon	10 mL
2 tsp	ground ginger	10 mL
2 tsp	ground cumin	10 mL
1/2 tsp	ground allspice	2 mL
1/4 tsp	freshly grated nutmeg	1 mL
1	large onion, chopped	1
1	can (14 oz/398 mL) diced tomatoes, with juice	1
1 tsp	salt	5 mL
1 cup	chicken broth or water	250 mL

1. In a skillet or wok, heat oil over medium-high heat. Add lamb, in batches, and brown on all sides, about 8 minutes per batch. Transfer to slow cooker stoneware as completed. Drain off all but 1 tbsp (15 mL) fat from pan.

2. Lower heat to medium. Add cinnamon, ginger, cumin, allspice and nutmeg to pan and stir-fry until fragrant, about 1 minute. Add onion and stir-fry until softened, about 3 minutes. Add tomatoes with juice and salt and bring to a boil, stirring and scraping up brown bits from bottom of pan.

3. Transfer to slow cooker stoneware and add broth. Cover and cook on Low for 10 hours or on High for 5 hours, until meat is falling off the bone. Serve immediately.

Lamb Biriyani

Tips

If you prefer a more gently spiced dish, reduce the quantity of cayenne.

To purée gingerroot, use a fine, sharp-toothed grater, such as those made by Microplane.

Use canned diced tomatoes. You'll need about half of a 14-oz (398 mL) can.

Preparation Time: 20 minutes, plus marinating
Medium (approx. 4 quart) slow cooker
Heat Rating: 🌶🌶

Lamb

½ cup	plain yogurt (not lower-fat)	125 mL
6 tbsp	finely chopped cilantro leaves	90 mL
4	cloves garlic, minced	4
1 tsp	puréed gingerroot (see Tips, left)	5 mL
1 lb	trimmed stewing lamb, cut into bite-size pieces	500 g
2 tbsp	oil	30 mL
1	onion, finely chopped	1
1 tbsp	ground coriander	15 mL
1 tsp	ground cumin	5 mL
1 tsp	ground turmeric	5 mL
1 tsp	cayenne pepper (see Tips, left)	5 mL
1 cup	diced tomatoes, with juice (see Tips, left)	250 mL
3 tbsp	warm milk	45 mL
1 tsp	saffron threads	5 mL

Rice

2 tbsp	oil	30 mL
1	onion, halved and thinly sliced	1
2 tsp	cumin seeds	10 mL
10	black peppercorns	10
6	cloves	6
4	green cardamom pods	4
1	piece (2 inches/5 cm) cinnamon stick	1
1 cup	long-grain parboiled (converted) white rice, preferably basmati (see Tip, page 43)	250 mL
	Butter	
2 cups	boiling water	500 mL

1. *Lamb:* In a bowl, combine yogurt, cilantro, garlic and ginger. Add lamb and toss until well coated. Cover and refrigerate for at least 4 or up to 6 hours.

2. In a skillet or wok, heat oil over medium heat. Add onion and stir-fry until lightly golden, about 12 minutes. Add coriander, cumin, turmeric and cayenne and stir-fry until fragrant, about 1 minute. Add lamb, with marinade, and stir-fry for 2 minutes. Stir in tomatoes and juice and bring to a boil. Remove from heat and set aside.

Tip

Be sure to use parboiled (also known as converted) rice. Because the process of parboiling keeps the kernels from sticking together, it works best in the slow cooker.

3. In a small bowl, combine warm milk and saffron. Set aside.

4. *Rice:* In a clean skillet, heat oil over medium heat. Add onion and stir-fry until softened, about 3 minutes. Add cumin, peppercorns, cloves, cardamom and cinnamon and stir-fry until very fragrant, about 2 minutes. Add rice and stir-fry until well coated with mixture. Remove from heat and set aside.

5. Lightly butter slow cooker stoneware. Spread a thin layer of lamb mixture over the bottom and cover evenly with half the rice mixture. Drizzle saffron milk evenly overtop. Spread remaining lamb mixture overtop and finish with remaining rice. Pour boiling water evenly overtop. Cover and cook on Low for 3 hours, until liquid is absorbed and rice fluffs easily with a fork. Discard cloves, cardamom and cinnamon and serve immediately.

Lamb-Spiked Mulligatawny Soup

Tips

If you prefer a spicier curry, substitute an equal quantity of hot curry paste for the mild.

Be sure to cut your potatoes into small pieces, about $1/4$ inch (0.5 cm). Otherwise they won't be cooked when the lamb is done.

If you prefer, shred the potatoes using the large holes of a box grater.

Preparation Time: 10 minutes, plus soaking
Medium (approx. 4 quart) slow cooker
Heat Rating: 🔥

$1/3$ cup	yellow split peas, rinsed and drained	75 mL
5 cups	boiling water, divided	1.25 L
2 tbsp	oil	30 mL
1	large onion, finely chopped	1
2	large carrots, peeled and diced	2
2	potatoes, peeled and diced (see Tips, left)	2
$1/3$ cup	long-grain parboiled (converted) white rice	75 mL
4 oz	trimmed stewing lamb, cut into bite-size pieces	125 g
2 tbsp	mild curry paste (see Tips, left)	30 mL
	Salt and freshly ground black pepper	
	Small bunch cilantro, chopped, plus additional leaves to garnish	

1. In a bowl, combine split peas with $1\frac{1}{4}$ cups (300 mL) boiling water. Set aside for 1 hour to soak. Drain.

2. In a large skillet or wok, heat oil over medium heat. Add onion and stir-fry until softened, about 4 minutes. Add carrots and potatoes and stir-fry for 1 minute. Add rice and lamb and toss to coat.

3. Transfer to slow cooker stoneware. Add curry paste and reserved split peas. Add remaining boiling water and mix well. Season to taste with salt and pepper.

4. Cover and cook on Low for 6 hours or on High for 3 hours, until peas are tender. Stir in cilantro. Garnish with additional cilantro leaves and serve immediately in warmed bowls.

Goat & Potato Curry

Serves 6

Tips

Serve this curry over a bed of rice.

Goat is very popular in India. In North America, look for it in specialty meat markets. Middle Eastern or Caribbean butcher shops are likely to have it.

Variations

Substitute stewing lamb or beef for the goat.

Preparation Time: 10 minutes, plus marinating
Medium (approx. 4 quart) slow cooker
Heat Rating: 🌶🌶

3 tbsp	ground coriander	45 mL
2 tbsp	ground turmeric	30 mL
2 tbsp	ground ginger	30 mL
2 tsp	ground cinnamon	10 mL
1 tsp	ground cardamom	5 mL
1 tsp	salt	5 mL
1 tsp	freshly ground black pepper	5 mL
½ tsp	ground fenugreek seeds	2 mL
1½ lbs	trimmed stewing goat, cut into 1-inch (2.5 cm) cubes and patted dry	750 g
2 tbsp	oil	30 mL
1	onion, sliced	1
2 cups	beef broth	500 mL
2	long red chile peppers, minced	2
3	large potatoes, peeled and diced	3

1. In a small bowl, combine coriander, turmeric, ginger, cinnamon, cardamom, salt, pepper and fenugreek. Mix well.

2. Place goat meat in a bowl. Add spice mixture and rub into the cubes of meat. Cover and refrigerate for at least 6 hours or overnight.

3. In a large skillet or wok, heat oil over medium-low heat. Add meat mixture and onion and cook, stirring, until meat is nicely browned, about 12 minutes.

4. Transfer to slow cooker stoneware. Add broth, chiles and potatoes. Cover and cook on Low for 8 hours or on High for 4 hours, until meat is very tender and potatoes are cooked through.

Poultry & Eggs

Bombay Chicken Curry

Tips

Serve this with an abundance of steaming basmati rice to soak up the sauce.

Be sure to shake the can of coconut milk well before using, because the cream layer collects on top after it's been sitting.

Preparation Time: 10 minutes
Medium (approx. 4 quart) slow cooker
Heat Rating: 🔥🔥

2 tbsp	oil	30 mL
2	onions, chopped	2
2	cloves garlic, minced	2
3 tbsp	medium curry powder	45 mL
1 tsp	ground ginger	5 mL
1 tsp	ground turmeric	5 mL
2 lbs	skinless bone-in chicken thighs (about 8)	1 kg
1	can (14 oz/398 mL) diced tomatoes, with juice	1
1	can (14 oz/400 mL) coconut milk (see Tips, left)	1
	Salt	

1. In a large skillet, heat oil over medium heat. Add onions and stir-fry until soft and beginning to turn golden, about 8 minutes. Add garlic, curry powder, ginger and turmeric and stir-fry until fragrant, about 1 minute. Add chicken and cook, stirring with a wooden spoon, until well coated with mixture and beginning to brown, about 4 minutes. Add tomatoes, with juice, and stir, scraping up brown bits from bottom of pan.

2. Transfer to slow cooker stoneware. Add coconut milk. Season to taste with salt and stir well. Cover and cook on Low for 4 hours or on High for 2 hours, until chicken is falling off the bone.

Chettinad Chicken

Serves 4

Tips

Serve with hot basmati rice and/or Indian bread.

If you can't find curry leaves, substitute dried or fresh bay leaves.

As noted, this recipe is fiery, particularly if you are using a hot curry paste. For a less incendiary dish, reduce the amount of curry powder or paste.

Preparation Time: 10 minutes
Medium (approx. 4 quart) slow cooker
Heat Rating: ♨♨♨

2 tbsp	oil or ghee	30 mL
2	bay leaves	2
8	green cardamom pods	8
1	piece (2 inches/5 cm) cinnamon stick	1
2 tsp	cumin seeds	10 mL
1 tsp	fennel seeds	5 mL
20	whole black peppercorns	20
6	dried red chile peppers	6
3	whole cloves	3
15	curry leaves	15
2	onions, finely chopped	2
¼ cup	Madras curry powder or paste (see Tips, left)	60 mL
1	tomato, chopped	1
2 lbs	skinless bone-in chicken thighs	1 kg
	Chicken broth	
	Plain yogurt	

1. In a skillet, heat oil over medium-high heat. Add bay leaves, cardamom pods, cinnamon, cumin and fennel seeds, peppercorns, chiles and cloves. Stir-fry until fragrant, about 2 minutes. Reduce heat to medium. Add curry leaves and onions and stir-fry until onions are lightly colored, about 8 minutes. Add curry powder or paste and stir-fry for 4 minutes, adding a bit of water to prevent sticking. Add tomato, with juices, and cook, stirring, for 1 minute, scraping up brown bits from bottom of pan.

2. Arrange chicken evenly over bottom of slow cooker stoneware. Add onion mixture and stir well. Add just enough chicken broth to cover. Cover and cook on Low for 6 hours or on High for 3 hours, until juices run clear when chicken is pierced with a fork. Serve immediately, with yogurt alongside.

Butter Chicken

Tips

Serve with an abundance of steaming basmati rice and warm naan bread to soak up the sauce.

If you prefer a milder result, reduce the quantity of cayenne.

Preparation Time: 25 minutes, plus marinating
Medium (approx. 4 quart) slow cooker
Heat Rating: ♨♨

1 cup	unsalted raw cashews	250 mL
1/4 cup	curry powder	60 mL
1 tbsp	fennel seeds	15 mL
2/3 cup	plain yogurt (not lower-fat)	150 mL
1/4 cup	tomato paste	60 mL
2 tbsp	white wine vinegar	30 mL
4	cloves garlic	4
1 tbsp	minced gingerroot	15 mL
2 lbs	skinless boneless chicken thighs, cut into 1-inch (2.5 cm) cubes	1 kg
1/4 cup	butter	60 mL
1	large onion, finely chopped	1
1	piece (about 4 inches/10 cm) cinnamon stick	1
4	green cardamom pods, crushed	4
1 tsp	cayenne pepper (see Tips, left)	5 mL
1	can (14 oz/398 mL) diced tomatoes, with juice	1
2/3 cup	chicken broth	150 mL
	Salt and freshly ground black pepper	
1/3 cup	table (18%) cream	75 mL
	Cilantro stems, optional	

1. In a dry skillet over medium heat, toast cashews, curry powder and fennel seeds, stirring, until fragrant, about 2 minutes. Transfer to a spice grinder and grind to a fine powder. Set aside.

2. In a blender or food processor fitted with the metal blade, process yogurt, tomato paste, vinegar, garlic, ginger and reserved cashew mixture until smooth and blended. Transfer to a large bowl. Add chicken, toss well, cover and refrigerate for 24 hours.

3. When you're ready to cook, in a large skillet, melt butter over medium heat. Add onion, cinnamon and cardamom pods and stir-fry until onion is softened, about 3 minutes. Add cayenne and tomatoes with juice and bring to a boil, stirring and scraping up brown bits from bottom of pan.

Tip

To serve four people: Cut the quantities in half and use a small (approx. 2 quart) slow cooker.

4. Transfer chicken, with marinade, to slow cooker stoneware. Add tomato mixture and chicken broth and stir well. Season to taste with salt and freshly ground pepper. Cover and cook on Low for 6 hours or on High for 3 hours, until juices run clear when chicken is pierced with a fork.

5. Add cream to stoneware and stir well. Cover and cook on Low for 10 minutes, to meld flavors. Garnish with cilantro stems, if using.

Goan Chicken Xacutti

Tips

As noted, this recipe is fiery. For a less incendiary dish, reduce the cayenne to $\frac{1}{4}$ to $\frac{1}{2}$ tsp (1 to 2 mL). You might also consider reducing the quantity of fresh chile peppers.

To purée garlic and gingerroot, use a fine, sharp-toothed grater, such as those made by Microplane.

Preparation Time: 20 minutes, plus marinating
Medium (approx. 4 quart) slow cooker
Heat Rating: ♨♨♨

Marinade

2 tbsp	finely chopped cilantro	30 mL
1 tbsp	puréed garlic (see Tips, left)	15 mL
1 tbsp	puréed gingerroot	15 mL
1 tbsp	tamarind paste (see Tips, page 53)	15 mL
1 tsp	ground turmeric	5 mL
1 tsp	cayenne pepper (see Tips, left)	5 mL
2 lbs	skinless bone-in chicken drumsticks and/or thighs	1 kg
2 tbsp	unsweetened shredded or desiccated coconut	30 mL
1 tbsp	oil	15 mL
2	onions, finely chopped	2
2 tbsp	garam masala	30 mL
1 tbsp	tomato paste	15 mL
4	long red chile peppers	4
1 tsp	ground cloves	5 mL
1	piece (4 inches/10 cm) cinnamon stick	1
2 cups	water	500 mL
	Chopped cilantro leaves	
	Lime wedges	

1. *Marinade:* In a large bowl, combine cilantro, garlic, ginger, tamarind paste, turmeric and cayenne (add a little warm water if necessary) to make a smooth paste. Add chicken and toss to coat well. Cover and refrigerate for at least 6 hours or overnight.

2. In a large, dry skillet, over low heat, toast coconut until lightly golden, about 3 minutes. Transfer to a small bowl and set aside.

Tip

Tip

Be sure to use tamarind paste (sometimes labeled "concentrate"), which comes in a jar. Tamarind in a block needs to be dissolved in water and pressed through a sieve to remove seeds and pulp before being added to recipes and, therefore, becomes more diluted in flavor and texture.

3. In the same skillet, heat oil over medium heat. Add onions and stir-fry until lightly browned, about 9 minutes. Stir in garam masala, tomato paste, chiles, cloves and cinnamon stick. Add water and stir well, scraping up brown bits from bottom of pan.

4. Transfer to slow cooker stoneware. Add chicken, with marinade, and stir well. Cover and cook on Low for 6 hours or on High for 3 hours, until juices run clear when chicken is pierced with a fork. Garnish with cilantro and serve immediately, accompanied by lime wedges for squeezing over.

Trivandrum Chicken & Coconut Curry

Serves 4

Tips

Serve this with plenty of basmati rice.

Use a quantity of chile peppers to suit your taste. If you are timid about heat, use only one, and seed and devein it before mincing.

Palm sugar is also known as jaggery. You can substitute raw cane sugar such as Mexican piloncillo, or regular dark brown sugar.

Preparation Time: 10 minutes
Medium (approx. 4 quart) slow cooker
Heat Rating:

2 tbsp	oil	30 mL
2	onions, finely chopped	2
4	cloves garlic, minced	4
1 tbsp	minced gingerroot	15 mL
1 to 2	long red chile peppers, finely minced (see Tips, left)	1 to 2
1	piece (4 inches/10 cm) cinnamon stick	1
1 tbsp	ground coriander	15 mL
2 tsp	ground cumin	10 mL
1 tsp	ground cardamom	5 mL
1 tsp	garam masala	5 mL
1/2 tsp	ground turmeric	2 mL
1 lb	skinless boneless chicken breasts, cut into 1-inch (2.5 cm) cubes	500 g
1	can (14 oz/398 mL) diced tomatoes, with juice	1
2 tsp	soft palm sugar (see Tips, left)	10 mL
1	can (14 oz/400 mL) coconut milk	1
	Salt	

1. In a large skillet, heat oil over low heat. Add onions and cook, stirring often, until golden, about 12 minutes. Add garlic, ginger, chiles, cinnamon stick, coriander, cumin, cardamom, garam masala and turmeric and stir-fry until fragrant, about 1 minute. Increase heat to high. Add chicken and stir-fry for 3 minutes. Stir in tomatoes, with juice, and sugar, scraping up brown bits from bottom of pan.

2. Transfer to slow cooker stoneware. Add coconut milk and stir well. Season to taste with salt. Cover and cook on Low for 4 hours or on High for 2 hours, until chicken is no longer pink. Serve immediately.

Bangladeshi Chicken Curry

Tips

Serve this over steaming basmati rice.

To purée garlic, use a fine, sharp-toothed grater, such as those made by Microplane.

The best way to grind the mustard seeds for this recipe is in a mortar. You can also use an electric spice grinder, but be careful not to grind them too finely — you do not want powdered seeds for this recipe.

Preparation Time: 15 minutes
Medium (approx. 4 quart) slow cooker
Heat Rating: 🌶🌶

2 tbsp	oil	30 mL
1	onion, halved lengthwise and thinly sliced	1
2 tsp	puréed garlic (see Tips, left)	10 mL
2 tsp	brown mustard seeds, coarsely ground (see Tips, left)	10 mL
2 tbsp	curry powder	30 mL
2 tsp	ground coriander	10 mL
2 cups	chicken broth or water	500 mL
1½ lbs	skinless boneless chicken thighs, cut into 1-inch (2.5 cm) cubes	750 g
16	cherry tomatoes	16

1. In a skillet, heat oil over medium heat. Add onion and stir-fry until softened, about 3 minutes. Add garlic and mustard seeds and stir-fry for 1 minute. Add curry powder and coriander and stir-fry until fragrant, about 2 minutes. Stir in chicken broth, scraping up brown bits from bottom of pan.

2. Transfer to slow cooker stoneware. Stir in chicken and cherry tomatoes. Cover and cook on Low for 6 hours or on High for 3 hours, until juices run clear when chicken is pierced with a fork. Serve immediately.

Bhoona Chicken Curry

Tips

Serve with steamed basmati rice.

To serve two people: Cut the quantities in half and use a small (approx. 2 quart) slow cooker.

To serve six people: Increase the quantities by half and use a large (approx. 5 quart) slow cooker.

Preparation Time: 10 minutes, plus marinating
Medium (approx. 4 quart) slow cooker
Heat Rating:

Marinade

½ cup	plain yogurt (not lower-fat)	125 mL
¼ cup	freshly squeezed lime juice	60 mL
2	cloves garlic, minced	2
3 tbsp	ground cumin	45 mL
2 tbsp	ground coriander	30 mL
1 tsp	ground cardamom	5 mL
1 tsp	salt	5 mL
½ tsp	cayenne pepper	2 mL
2 lbs	skinless bone-in chicken thighs (about 8)	1 kg
1 tsp	garam masala	5 mL
	Handful of cilantro leaves, coarsely chopped	

1. *Marinade:* In a large bowl, combine yogurt, lime juice, garlic, cumin, coriander, cardamom, salt and cayenne. Add chicken and toss to coat thoroughly. Cover and refrigerate for 2 hours.

2. Transfer chicken, with marinade, to slow cooker stoneware. Cover and cook on Low for 6 hours or on High for 3 hours, until juices run clear when chicken is pierced with a fork. Stir in garam masala and cilantro and serve immediately.

Chicken & Spinach Curry

Serves 6

Tips

To purée garlic and gingerroot, use a fine, sharp-toothed grater, such as those made by Microplane.

To serve three people: Cut the quantities in half and use a small (approx. 2 quart) slow cooker.

To serve nine people: Increase the quantities by half and use a large (approx. 5 quart) slow cooker.

Preparation Time: 15 minutes, plus marinating
Medium (approx. 4 quart) slow cooker
Heat Rating: ♨♨

Marinade

¼ cup	plain yogurt (not lower-fat)	60 mL
1 tbsp	puréed garlic (see Tips, left)	15 mL
1 tbsp	puréed gingerroot	15 mL
1 tbsp	curry powder	15 mL
	Salt and freshly ground black pepper	
1½ lbs	skinless boneless chicken thighs, cut into 1-inch (2.5 cm) cubes	750 g
2 tbsp	oil	30 mL
1	onion, finely chopped	1
2 tsp	cumin seeds	10 mL
1 cup	chicken broth or water	250 mL
1 lb	fresh spinach, stems removed, or 1 package (10 oz/300 g) spinach leaves, thawed if frozen	500 g
1 tbsp	freshly squeezed lemon juice	15 mL

1. *Marinade:* In a large bowl, combine yogurt, garlic, ginger and curry powder. Season to taste with salt and freshly ground pepper. Add chicken and toss to mix well. Cover and refrigerate for at least 8 hours or overnight.

2. In a large skillet, heat oil over medium heat. Add onion and stir-fry until softened, about 3 minutes. Add cumin seeds and stir-fry until fragrant, about 1 minute. Add chicken mixture and stir-fry until well coated. Stir in chicken broth, scraping up brown bits from bottom of pan.

3. Transfer to slow cooker stoneware. Cover and cook on Low for 5 hours or on High for 2½ hours. Add spinach in batches, stirring after each addition, until all the leaves are submerged in the liquid. Stir in lemon juice. Cover and cook on High for 10 minutes, until spinach is wilted and flavors have melded.

Chicken Korma

Tips

Serve this with plain yogurt as a garnish and mounds of steaming basmati rice.

To serve two people: Cut the quantities in half and use a small (approx. 2 quart) slow cooker.

To serve six people: Increase the quantities by half and use a large (approx. 5 quart) slow cooker.

Preparation Time: 5 minutes
Medium (approx. 4 quart) slow cooker
Heat Rating: ♨

2 tbsp	oil	30 mL
1	onion, chopped	1
2	cloves garlic, crushed	2
1 lb	ground chicken	500 g
8 oz	potatoes, peeled and cut into ½-inch (1 cm) cubes	250 g
1 tbsp	korma curry paste or powder	15 mL
1 cup	chicken or vegetable broth	250 mL
2 tbsp	mango chutney	30 mL
	Salt and freshly ground black pepper	
	Chopped cilantro leaves	

1. In a skillet, heat oil over medium heat. Add onion and garlic and stir-fry until onion is starting to color, about 5 minutes. Add chicken and potatoes and stir-fry until chicken begins to brown, about 5 minutes. Stir in korma paste, then broth, scraping up brown bits from bottom of pan.

2. Transfer to slow cooker stoneware. Add chutney and season to taste with salt and freshly ground pepper. Cover and cook on Low for 6 hours or on High for 3 hours. Serve immediately, garnished with cilantro.

Creamy Kofta Curry

Tips

Serve with basmati rice and/ or Indian bread such as naan.

To purée garlic and gingerroot, use a fine, sharp-toothed grater, such as those made by Microplane.

To serve three people: Cut the quantities in half and use a small (approx. 2 quart) slow cooker.

To serve nine people: Increase the quantities by half and use a large (approx. 5 quart) slow cooker.

Preparation Time: 20 minutes, plus chilling
Medium (approx. 4 quart) slow cooker
Heat Rating: ♨♨

1¾ lbs	ground chicken	875 g
1 tbsp	puréed garlic (see Tips, left)	15 mL
1 tbsp	puréed gingerroot	15 mL
1 tsp	ground cinnamon	5 mL
¼ cup	finely chopped cilantro leaves, plus additional to garnish	60 mL
	Salt and freshly ground black pepper	
2 tbsp (approx.)	oil	30 mL
1	onion, finely chopped	1
2 tbsp	medium curry powder	30 mL
1	can (14 oz/398 mL) diced tomatoes, with juice	1
1 cup	chicken broth	250 mL
1 cup	table (18%) cream	250 mL

1. In a bowl, combine chicken, garlic, ginger, cinnamon and cilantro. Season to taste with salt and freshly ground pepper. Mix well and shape into walnut-sized balls. Place on a baking sheet, cover and refrigerate for at least 1 hour or up to 2 hours.

2. In a skillet, heat oil over medium-high heat. Add chicken balls, in batches, and stir-fry until lightly browned, about 5 minutes a batch, adding more oil if necessary. Using a slotted spoon, transfer to slow cooker as completed, arranging in a single layer.

3. Lower heat to medium. Add onion to pan and stir-fry until softened, about 3 minutes. Add curry powder and stir-fry until fragrant, about 2 minutes. Stir in tomatoes and broth, scraping up brown bits from bottom of pan. Season to taste with salt and freshly ground pepper. Pour over chicken balls.

4. Cover and cook on Low for 6 hours or on High for 3 hours, until mixture is hot and bubbly and juices run clear when meatballs are pierced with a fork. Stir in cream. Cover and cook on High for 10 minutes, until flavors meld.

Chicken Balti

Serves 4

Tips

Serve with basmati rice or warm naan.

If you can't find curry leaves, substitute dried or fresh bay leaves.

To serve two people: Cut the quantities in half and use a small (approx. 2 quart) slow cooker.

To serve six people: Increase the quantities by half and use a large (approx. 5 quart) slow cooker.

Preparation time: 15 minutes
Medium (approx. 4 quart) slow cooker
Heat Rating: ♨♨ to ♨♨♨

3 tbsp	oil	45 mL
1 lb	ground chicken	500 g
2	onions, thinly sliced	2
8	curry leaves (see Tips, left)	8
3	cloves garlic, minced	3
1 tbsp	minced gingerroot	15 mL
2 tbsp	medium or hot curry powder	30 mL
1 tbsp	ground coriander	15 mL
4	tomatoes, coarsely chopped	4
1 cup	chicken broth	250 mL
1¼ cups	sweet green peas, thawed if frozen	300 mL
2	long red chile peppers, seeded and thinly sliced	2
3 tbsp	freshly squeezed lemon juice	45 mL
	Small handful of chopped mint leaves	
	Small handful of chopped cilantro leaves	
	Salt	

1. In a skillet, heat oil over medium heat. Add chicken, onions and curry leaves and cook until chicken is no longer pink and onions are soft, about 5 minutes. Add garlic, ginger, curry powder and coriander and cook, stirring, for 1 minute. Stir in tomatoes and broth, scraping up brown bits from bottom of pan.

2. Transfer to slow cooker stoneware. Cover and cook on Low for 6 hours or on High for 3 hours. Stir in peas and chiles. Cover and cook on High for 10 minutes, until peas are tender. Stir in lemon juice, mint and cilantro and season to taste with salt. Serve immediately.

Thai Chicken Meatball Curry

Tips

As noted, this recipe is fiery. If you prefer a less incendiary dish, reduce the quantity of chile peppers in the meatballs and/or the quantity of curry paste in the sauce.

Before chopping, remove and discard the tough outer layers of the lemongrass.

Preparation Time: 20 minutes
Medium (approx. 4 quart) slow cooker
Heat Rating: ◊◊◊

1¾ lbs	ground chicken	875 g
⅔ cup	fresh bread crumbs	150 mL
¾ cup	chopped cilantro, divided	175 mL
¼ cup	finely chopped lemongrass	60 mL
3	long red chile peppers, minced (see Tips, left)	3
2 tbsp	oil, divided	30 mL
1	can (14 oz/400 mL) coconut milk	1
2 tbsp	Thai red curry paste (see Tips, left)	30 mL
1 tbsp	tomato paste	15 mL
	Salt and freshly ground black pepper	

1. In a large bowl, combine chicken, bread crumbs, half of the cilantro, lemongrass and chiles. Mix well and shape into walnut-sized balls.

2. In a large skillet or wok, heat 1 tbsp (15 mL) of the oil over medium-high heat. Add meatballs, in batches, and sauté, turning carefully, until nicely browned, about 4 minutes a batch. Transfer to slow cooker stoneware as completed, arranging in a single layer, and add remaining oil to pan as needed. Remove from heat.

3. Add coconut milk, curry paste and tomato paste to pan and stir well, scraping up brown bits from bottom. Pour over meatballs. Season to taste with salt and freshly ground black pepper.

4. Cover and cook on Low for 6 hours or on High for 3 hours, until meatballs are cooked through. Serve immediately, garnished with remaining cilantro.

Thai Yellow Chicken Curry

Tips

Serve with plenty of fragrant jasmine rice. For extra nutrition, use the brown variety.

Before chopping, remove and discard the tough outer layers of the lemongrass.

This produces a very hot curry. If you prefer a milder result, reduce the quantity of cayenne or fresh chile peppers.

Palm sugar is also known as jaggery. You can substitute raw cane sugar such as Mexican piloncillo, or regular dark brown sugar.

To serve two people: Cut the quantities in half and use a small (approx. 2 quart) slow cooker.

To serve six people: Increase the quantities by half and use a large (approx. 5 quart) slow cooker.

Preparation Time: 15 minutes
Medium (approx. 4 quart) slow cooker
Heat Rating: 🌶🌶🌶

2	shallots, coarsely chopped	2
4	wild lime leaves (see Tips, page 63)	4
2 tbsp	finely chopped lemongrass (see Tips, left)	2
2	long red or Thai bird's-eye chile peppers, coarsely chopped	2
3	cloves garlic, chopped	3
1 tbsp	finely chopped gingerroot	15 mL
1 tbsp	soft palm sugar (see Tips, left)	15 mL
2 tsp	turmeric	10 mL
1 tsp	cayenne pepper (see Tips, left)	5 mL
1 tsp	ground coriander	5 mL
1 tsp	ground cumin	5 mL
1/4 tsp	ground cinnamon	1 mL
1	can (14 oz/400 mL) coconut milk	1
3 tbsp	fish sauce	45 mL
1 tbsp	freshly squeezed lime juice	15 mL
2 lbs	skinless bone-in chicken drumsticks or thighs (about 8)	1 kg
8 oz	baby new potatoes, peeled and halved	250 g
12	Thai sweet basil leaves	12

1. In a food processor fitted with the metal blade, process shallots, lime leaves, lemongrass, chiles, garlic, gingerroot, palm sugar, turmeric, cayenne, coriander, cumin, cinnamon, coconut milk, fish sauce and lime juice until smooth and blended.

2. Arrange chicken evenly over bottom of slow cooker stoneware. Sprinkle potatoes evenly overtop. Cover and cook on Low for 6 hours or on High for 3 hours, until chicken is falling off the bone and potatoes are tender. Garnish with basil leaves and serve immediately.

Thai Green Chicken Curry

Serves 6

Tips

Serve in warm bowls with steamed jasmine rice.

As noted, this recipe is fiery. For a less incendiary dish, reduce the quantity of curry paste. You might also consider reducing the quantity of fresh chile peppers.

Substitute long red (cayenne) chile peppers for the green, if you prefer.

Palm sugar is also known as jaggery. You can substitute raw cane sugar such as Mexican piloncillo, or regular dark brown sugar.

Often called Kaffir lime leaves, wild lime leaves are the leaves of a small Asian lime. You can use fresh or frozen varieties. If you can't find them, in this recipe substitute 1 tbsp (15 mL) finely grated lime zest.

If you don't like green beans that are well-cooked, use sliced frozen (unthawed) beans in this recipe. Add the chicken to the pan in Step 1 and stir-fry for 2 minutes before adding the broth, to ensure that it cooks properly within the time frame, since the frozen beans will cool the mixture.

Preparation Time: 10 minutes
Medium (approx. 4 quart) slow cooker
Heat Rating: 🔥🔥🔥

1 tbsp	oil	15 mL
3 tbsp	Thai green curry paste (see Tips, left)	45 mL
2	long green chile peppers, finely chopped	2
6	wild lime leaves (see Tips, left)	6
1 tbsp	soft palm sugar (see Tips, left)	15 mL
8 oz	pea (Thai baby) eggplant or 1 small eggplant, cut into bite-sized cubes	250 g
1 cup	chicken broth	250 mL
1½ lbs	skinless boneless chicken thighs, cut into 1-inch (2.5 cm) cubes	750 g
1	can (14 oz/400 mL) coconut milk	1
2 tbsp	fish sauce, such as nam pla	30 mL
1 cup	sliced green beans (see Tips, left)	250 g
½ cup	canned bamboo shoots, rinsed and drained	125 mL
	Large handful of Thai sweet basil leaves	
	Large handful of cilantro leaves	
	Juice of 1 lime	

1. In a large skillet or wok, heat oil over medium-high heat. Add curry paste and chile peppers and stir-fry for 3 minutes. Add lime leaves, sugar and eggplant and stir-fry for 1 minute. Stir in chicken broth, scraping up brown bits from bottom of pan.

2. Transfer to slow cooker stoneware. Stir in chicken, coconut milk, fish sauce, green beans and bamboo shoots. Cover and cook on Low for 5 hours or on High for 2½ hours. Stir in basil, cilantro and lime juice and serve immediately.

Chicken Massaman

Serves 6

Tips

Serve with steamed Thai or jasmine rice.

Massaman curry paste is available in well-stocked Asian markets or online.

You can use 1 can (14 oz/400 mL) coconut milk which will be a bit less than the recipe calls for. Be sure to shake the can well before using, as the cream layer collects on the top after it's been sitting.

Preparation time: 10 minutes
Medium (approx. 4 quart) slow cooker
Heat Rating:

1 tbsp	oil	15 mL
1	large onion, halved lengthwise and thinly sliced	1
6 tbsp	massaman curry paste (see Tips, left)	90 mL
2 cups	coconut milk, divided (see Tips, left)	500 mL
1½ lbs	skinless boneless chicken thighs, cut into 1-inch (2.5 cm) cubes	750 g
2 tbsp	fish sauce, such as nam pla	30 mL
2 tbsp	freshly squeezed lime juice	30 mL
1 tsp	granulated sugar	5 mL
1	small Asian eggplant, cubed	1
2 tbsp	chopped Thai sweet basil	30 mL

1. In a skillet, heat oil over medium heat. Add onion and stir-fry until turning golden, about 8 minutes. Add curry paste and half of the coconut milk and stir well.

2. Transfer to slow cooker stoneware. Add chicken, fish sauce, lime juice, sugar, eggplant and remaining coconut milk and stir well.

3. Cover and cook on Low for 5 hours or on High for 2½ hours, until juices run clear when chicken is pierced with a fork. Stir in basil and serve immediately.

Balinese Mango & Chicken Curry

Serves 6

Tips

Candlenuts, also known as Indian walnuts, are called kukui nuts in Hawaii. Do not eat them raw. If you can't find them, substitute Brazil or macadamia nuts.

Palm sugar is also known as jaggery. You can substitute raw cane sugar such as Mexican piloncillo, or regular dark brown sugar.

To serve three people: Cut the quantities in half and use a small (approx. 2 quart) slow cooker.

To serve nine people: Increase the quantities by half and use a large (approx. 5 quart) slow cooker.

Preparation Time: 15 minutes, plus standing
Medium (approx. 4 quart) slow cooker
Heat Rating: ♨♨

2	green mangoes, peeled, pitted and cut into thin matchsticks	2
½ tsp	salt	2 mL
1 tsp	whole black peppercorns	5 mL
4	candlenuts (see Tips, left)	4
2	long red chile peppers, coarsely chopped	2
1¾ cups	water or chicken broth	425 mL
1 tsp	soft palm sugar (see Tips, left)	5 mL
1½ lbs	skinless boneless chicken, cut into 2-inch pieces	750 g
1 tbsp	freshly squeezed lime juice	15 mL
1 cup	coconut milk	250 mL
3 tbsp	chopped mint leaves	45 mL

1. In a colander placed over a sink, combine mangoes and salt. Set aside to "sweat" for 20 minutes. Squeeze out moisture and set aside.

2. In a mortar, using a pestle, crush peppercorns. Add candlenuts and crush. Add chiles and continue crushing until mixture forms a rough paste.

3. In a bowl, combine water and palm sugar. Add candlenut paste and mix well.

4. Arrange chicken evenly over bottom of slow cooker stoneware. Top with reserved mangoes and sprinkle lime juice evenly overtop. Pour candlenut mixture evenly overtop.

5. Cover and cook on Low for 5 hours or on High for 2½ hours. Add coconut milk. Cover and cook on High for 10 minutes to meld flavors. Serve immediately, garnished with mint.

Singapore Chicken Curry

Preparation Time: 15 minutes
Medium (approx. 4 quart) slow cooker
Heat Rating: 🔥🔥

Serves 6

Tips

Remove the tough outer layers of lemongrass and cut the remaining stalk into several sections. Using the flat side of the knife, smash each piece (this helps to release the flavor).

Often called Kaffir lime leaves, wild lime leaves are the leaves of a small Asian lime. You can use fresh or frozen varieties. If you can't find them, in this recipe substitute 2 tsp (10 mL) finely grated lime zest.

Be sure to use tamarind paste (sometimes labeled "concentrate"), which comes in a jar. Tamarind in a block needs to be dissolved in water and pressed through a sieve to remove seeds and pulp before being added to recipes and, therefore, becomes more diluted in flavor and texture.

When using canned coconut milk, be sure to shake well before using, because the cream layer collects on the top after it's been sitting.

2	onions, quartered	2
6	cloves garlic, coarsely chopped	6
1	piece (2 inches/5 cm) peeled gingerroot, quartered	1
½ cup	water	125 mL
¼ cup	oil	60 mL
6 tbsp	medium curry powder	90 mL
2	stalks lemongrass, smashed (see Tips, left)	2
8	wild lime leaves (see Tips, left)	8
1 tbsp	tamarind paste (see Tips, left)	15 mL
1	can (14 oz/400 mL) coconut milk	1
1¾ lbs	skinless boneless chicken thighs, cut into 1-inch (2.5 cm) cubes	875 g
1 lb	potatoes, peeled and cut into bite-sized pieces	500 g
	Salt and freshly ground black pepper	
	Small handful of chopped cilantro	

1. In a food processor fitted with the metal blade, process onions, garlic, ginger and water until a smooth paste forms.

2. In a skillet, heat oil over medium heat. Add onion paste and stir-fry for 4 minutes. Add curry powder and stir-fry for 2 minutes, until fragrant. Add lemongrass, lime leaves and tamarind paste and stir well. Stir in coconut milk. Remove from heat and set aside.

3. Arrange chicken evenly over bottom of slow cooker stoneware. Scatter potatoes evenly overtop. Add coconut milk mixture and stir well. Season to taste with salt and freshly ground pepper.

4. Cover and cook on Low for 6 hours or on high for 3 hours, until juices run clear when chicken is pierced with a fork. Stir in cilantro and serve immediately.

Malaysian Chicken Curry

Tips

Thai shallots are round and quite a bit smaller than those commonly available in North America. If you can't find them, use half the quantity of the larger, longer variety.

To serve two people: Cut the quantities in half and use a small (approx. 2 quart) slow cooker.

To serve six people: Increase the quantities by half and use a large (approx. 5 quart) slow cooker.

Preparation Time: 10 minutes, plus marinating
Medium (approx. 4 quart) slow cooker
Heat Rating: ♨♨

Marinade

10	Thai shallots, coarsely chopped (see Tips, left)	10
1	piece (2 inches/5 cm) gingerroot, peeled and coarsely chopped	1
2	cloves garlic, coarsely chopped	2
2 lbs	skinless bone-in chicken thighs (8 thighs)	1 kg

Curry

2 tbsp	oil	30 mL
10	Thai shallots, finely chopped	10
1	piece (4 inches/10 cm) cinnamon stick	1
2	whole cloves	2
2	star anise	2
2 tbsp	medium curry paste	30 mL
2	large potatoes, peeled and diced	2
1¼ cups	coconut milk	300 mL

1. *Marinade:* In a food processor fitted with the metal blade, process shallots, ginger and garlic until a smooth paste forms. Place chicken in one layer in a shallow dish, spread with paste and set aside at room temperature for 20 minutes.

2. *Curry:* In a large skillet or wok, heat oil over medium-high heat. Add shallots, cinnamon, cloves and star anise and stir-fry until fragrant, about 3 minutes. Add curry paste and stir-fry for 3 minutes. Add chicken, with marinade, and stir-fry for 4 minutes.

3. Transfer to slow cooker stoneware. Scatter potatoes evenly over chicken and add coconut milk. Cover and cook on Low for 6 hours or on High for 3 hours, until potatoes are tender and juices run clear when chicken is pierced with a fork.

Filipino Chicken Adobo

Tips

Serve with plenty of steamed rice.

If you enjoy the taste of garlic, feel free to increase the quantity to as many as 20 cloves.

To serve two people: Cut the quantities in half and use a small (approx. 2 quart) slow cooker.

To serve six people: Increase the quantities by half and use a large (approx. 5 quart) slow cooker.

Preparation Time: 10 minutes
Medium (approx. 4 quart) slow cooker
Heat Rating: ♨

Adobo Stock

½ cup	apple cider vinegar	125 mL
½ cup	soy sauce	125 mL
2 cups	chicken broth	500 mL
2	bay leaves	2
1 tsp	freshly ground black pepper	5 mL
2 tbsp	oil	30 mL
15	cloves garlic, coarsely chopped (see Tips, left)	15
2 lbs	skinless bone-in chicken thighs	1 kg

1. *Adobo Stock:* In a saucepan, combine vinegar, soy sauce, chicken broth, bay leaves and pepper. Bring to a boil over medium-high heat. Reduce heat and simmer for 20 minutes.

2. In a skillet, heat oil over medium heat. Add garlic and stir-fry just until it begins to turn golden, about 6 minutes. Be careful not to let it burn. Add adobo stock and stir well.

3. Arrange chicken evenly over bottom of slow cooker stoneware. Add adobo mixture. Cover and cook on Low for 6 hours or on High for 3 hours, until juices run clear when chicken is pierced with a fork. Remove and discard bay leaves and serve immediately.

Mandalay Chicken Curry

Tips

Serve with plenty of hot rice.

Coconut cream is a thicker, more concentrated version of coconut milk. Look for it in Asian markets. If you can't find it, skim off the top layer of a can of coconut milk that has been left standing (do not shake it).

Preparation Time: 5 minutes
Medium (approx. 4 quart) slow cooker
Heat Rating: 🌶🌶

1 lb	skinless boneless chicken breasts, cut into 1-inch (2.5 cm) cubes	500 g
1	can (13 oz/400 g) bamboo shoots, rinsed and drained	1
¼ cup	coconut cream (see Tips, left)	60 mL
2 tbsp	medium curry paste	30 mL
1 tbsp	oil	15 mL
1 tsp	ground turmeric	5 mL
1 tsp	shrimp paste	5 mL
	Chicken broth or water	
	Salt and freshly ground black pepper	
	Lime wedges	

1. In slow cooker stoneware, combine chicken and bamboo shoots. Stir well.

2. In a small bowl, combine coconut cream, curry paste, oil, turmeric, and shrimp paste. Mix well and pour over chicken. Add chicken broth barely to cover and season to taste with salt and freshly ground pepper.

3. Cover and cook on Low for 6 hours or on High for 3 hours, until chicken is no longer pink. Serve immediately with lime wedges for squeezing over.

Spicy Coconut Chicken Curry

Serves 4

Tips

Serve this with plenty of steaming rice to soak up the sauce. Chutney or Indian pickle adds a pleasant accent.

To serve two people: Cut the quantities in half and use a small (approx. 2 quart) slow cooker.

To serve six people: Increase the quantities by half and use a large (approx. 5 quart) slow cooker.

Preparation Time: 10 minutes, plus marinating
Medium (approx. 4 quart) slow cooker
Heat Rating: 🌶🌶🌶

2 lbs	skinless bone-in chicken drumsticks or thighs	1 kg
3 tbsp	hot curry powder	45 mL
2 tbsp	oil	30 mL
1	onion, thinly sliced	1
4	cloves garlic, minced	4
4	tomatoes, chopped	4
2	chicken bouillon cubes, crumbled	2
3 cups	coconut milk	750 mL
3	potatoes, peeled and diced	3
	Finely chopped cilantro leaves	

1. Place chicken in a non-reactive bowl or baking dish. Sprinkle curry powder evenly overtop and toss to mix well. Cover and refrigerate for 30 minutes.

2. In a skillet, heat oil over medium heat. Add onion and stir-fry until softened, about 3 minutes. Add garlic and tomatoes and stir-fry for 2 minutes. Add bouillon cubes and stir well. Stir in coconut milk.

3. Arrange chicken evenly over bottom of slow cooker stoneware. Sprinkle potatoes evenly overtop. Add tomato mixture.

4. Cover and cook on Low for 6 hours or on High for 3 hours, until chicken is very tender and potatoes are cooked through. Serve immediately, garnished with cilantro.

Penang Red Chicken Curry

Tips

Serve with steamed jasmine rice.

Two chile peppers plus 1 tsp (5 mL) cayenne produces a fiery curry. If you prefer a milder result, use just one chile and reduce the quantity of cayenne.

Often called Kaffir lime leaves, wild lime leaves are the leaves of a small Asian lime. You can use fresh or frozen varieties. If you can't find them, in this recipe substitute 1 tsp (5 mL) finely grated lime zest.

Preparation Time: 10 minutes
Medium (approx. 4 quart) slow cooker
Heat Rating: ♨♨♨

Penang Red Curry Paste

1	can (14 oz/400 mL) coconut milk	1
1/4 cup	tomato paste	60 mL
2 tbsp	soy sauce	30 mL
2 tbsp	fish sauce	30 mL
1 tbsp	freshly squeezed lime juice	15 mL
1	small onion, quartered	1
1	piece (2 inches/5 cm) peeled gingerroot, quartered	1
3	cloves garlic, coarsely chopped	3
2	wild lime leaves (see Tips, left)	2
1 to 2	long red chile pepper(s) (see Tips, left)	1 to 2
1 tsp	shrimp paste	5 mL
2 tbsp	ground coriander	30 mL
1 tbsp	ground cumin	15 mL
1 tbsp	sweet paprika	15 mL
1 tsp	cayenne pepper	5 mL
1/2 tsp	ground turmeric	2 mL
1/2 tsp	ground cinnamon	2 mL
1/4 tsp	ground nutmeg	1 mL
1/4 tsp	ground cloves	1 mL
2 lbs	skinless bone-in chicken drumsticks or thighs	1 kg
3	tomatoes, cut into wedges	3
2	red bell peppers, sliced lengthwise, seeded and thinly sliced	2
	Thai sweet basil leaves	

1. *Penang Red Curry Paste:* In a food processor fitted with the metal blade, process coconut milk, tomato paste, soy sauce, fish sauce, lime juice, onion, ginger, garlic, lime leaves, chiles, shrimp paste, coriander, cumin, paprika, cayenne, turmeric, cinnamon, nutmeg and cloves, until smoothly blended. Set aside.

2. Arrange chicken evenly over bottom of slow cooker stoneware and scatter tomatoes overtop. Add curry paste. Cover and cook on Low for 6 hours or on High for 3 hours, until juices run clear when pierced with a fork. Add bell peppers. Cover and cook on High for 15 minutes, until peppers are tender. Garnish with basil leaves and serve immediately.

Burmese-Style Tomato & Chicken Curry

Tips

Serve with steaming jasmine rice.

Palm sugar is also known as jaggery. You can substitute raw cane sugar such as Mexican piloncillo, or regular dark brown sugar.

To serve two people: Cut the quantities in half and use a small (approx. 2 quart) slow cooker.

To serve six people: Increase the quantities by half and use a large (approx. 5 quart) slow cooker.

Preparation Time: 10 minutes
Medium (approx. 4 quart) slow cooker
Heat Rating: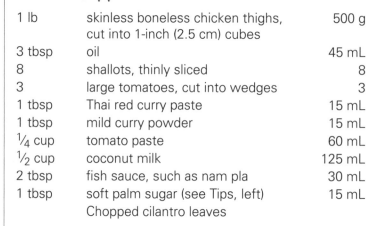

1 lb	skinless boneless chicken thighs, cut into 1-inch (2.5 cm) cubes	500 g
3 tbsp	oil	45 mL
8	shallots, thinly sliced	8
3	large tomatoes, cut into wedges	3
1 tbsp	Thai red curry paste	15 mL
1 tbsp	mild curry powder	15 mL
¼ cup	tomato paste	60 mL
½ cup	coconut milk	125 mL
2 tbsp	fish sauce, such as nam pla	30 mL
1 tbsp	soft palm sugar (see Tips, left)	15 mL
	Chopped cilantro leaves	

1. Arrange chicken evenly over bottom of slow cooker stoneware.

2. In a skillet, heat oil over low heat. Add shallots and stir-fry until soft and lightly golden, about 7 minutes. Using a slotted spoon, transfer to slow cooker stoneware, spreading evenly over chicken. Arrange tomato wedges evenly over mixture.

3. Return skillet to low heat. Add curry paste and curry powder and cook, stirring, for 1 minute. Add tomato paste and stir well. Stir in coconut milk, fish sauce and palm sugar. Pour over chicken. Add water to barely cover chicken.

4. Cover and cook on Low for 6 hours or on High for 3 hours, until chicken is meltingly tender. Serve immediately, garnished with cilantro.

Burmese Chicken & Shrimp Curry

Tips

This recipe is particularly delicious served over hot rice noodles.

Shrimp paste, which is made from ground dried fermented shrimp, is available in Asian markets. It lends saltiness and depth of flavor to sauces. If you can't find it, in this recipe substitute one mashed anchovy fillet or 1 tsp (5 mL) anchovy paste.

Preparation time: 15 minutes
Medium (approx. 4 quart) slow cooker
Heat Rating:

2	large onions, coarsely chopped	2
5	cloves garlic, coarsely chopped	5
1 tbsp	coarsely chopped peeled gingerroot	15 mL
2 tbsp	oil	30 mL
½ tsp	shrimp paste (see Tips, left)	2 mL
2 tbsp	medium curry powder	30 mL
1¾ lb	skinless boneless chicken thighs, cut into 1-inch (2.5 cm) cubes	875 g
1	can (14 oz/400 mL) coconut milk	1
	Salt and freshly ground black pepper	
8 oz	peeled, deveined shrimp, cut into bite-sized pieces	250 g
	Chopped cilantro leaves	
	Sliced red chile peppers	
	Lime wedges	

1. In a food processor fitted with the metal blade, process onions, garlic and ginger until a smooth paste forms, stopping and scraping down the sides of the work bowl as necessary. (Add a little water if required.)

2. In a large skillet, heat oil over medium-high heat. Add onion mixture and shrimp paste and cook, stirring, for about 5 minutes. Stir in curry powder. Add chicken and cook, stirring, for 5 minutes.

3. Transfer to slow cooker stoneware. Add coconut milk and season to taste with salt and freshly ground pepper. Cover and cook on Low for 3 hours or on High for 1½ hours. Add shrimp and stir well. Cover and cook on High until shrimp are pink and opaque, about 20 minutes. Serve immediately, garnished with cilantro and/or chile peppers, and with lime wedges for squeezing over.

Indonesian Chicken Curry

Serves 6

Tips

Serve with steamed jasmine rice.

Candlenuts, also known as Indian walnuts, are called kukui nuts in Hawaii. Do not eat them raw. If you can't find them, substitute Brazil or macadamia nuts.

Shrimp paste is available in Asian markets. It adds depth and a hint of intriguing flavor to the sauce.

Be sure to use tamarind paste (sometimes labeled "concentrate"), which comes in a jar. Tamarind in a block needs to be dissolved in water and pressed through a sieve to remove seeds and pulp before being added to recipes and, therefore, becomes more diluted in flavor and texture.

Palm sugar is also known as jaggery. You can substitute raw cane sugar such as Mexican piloncillo, or regular dark brown sugar.

Preparation Time: 15 minutes
Medium (approx. 4 quart) slow cooker
Heat Rating: 🌶🌶

½	large onion, coarsely chopped	½
2 tbsp	finely chopped lemongrass	30 mL
3	cloves garlic, coarsely chopped	3
5	candlenuts (see Tips, left)	5
1 tbsp	minced gingerroot	15 mL
2	long red chile peppers	2
1 tbsp	ground coriander	15 mL
1 tsp	fennel seeds	5 mL
1 tsp	shrimp paste	5 mL
1	can (14 oz/400 mL) coconut milk	1
1 tbsp	tamarind paste (see Tips, left)	15 mL
1 tsp	salt	5 mL
1 tsp	soft palm sugar (see Tips, left)	5 mL
1½ lbs	skinless boneless chicken thighs, cut into 1-inch (2.5 cm) cubes	750 g
2	wild lime leaves (see Tips, page 71)	2
2 tbsp	unsweetened flaked or desiccated coconut	30 mL

1. In a food processor fitted with the metal blade, pulse onion, lemongrass, garlic, candlenuts, ginger, chiles, coriander, fennel seeds and shrimp paste until chopped and blended. Add coconut milk, tamarind paste, salt and sugar and process until smoothly blended, stopping and scraping down sides of the work bowl as necessary.

2. Arrange chicken evenly over bottom of slow cooker stoneware. Add coconut milk mixture and lime leaves. Cover and cook on Low for 6 hours or on High for 3 hours, until juices run clear when chicken is pierced with a fork.

3. In a small skillet over medium heat, toast coconut until lightly golden, about 3 minutes. Sprinkle over curry and serve immediately.

Chicken & Red Lentil Curry

Tips

Serve in individual bowls with basmati rice.

If you are a heat seeker, add a bit (up to $\frac{1}{2}$ tsp/2 mL) of cayenne pepper along with the curry powder.

Coconut cream is a thicker, more concentrated version of coconut milk. Look for it in Asian markets. If you can't find it, skim off the top layer of a can of coconut milk that has been left standing (do not shake it).

Preparation Time: 15 minutes, plus soaking
Medium (approx. 4 quart) slow cooker
Heat Rating: ♨♨

¾ cup	split red lentils, picked over and rinsed	175 mL
2 tbsp	oil	30 mL
2	onions, thinly sliced	2
2	cloves garlic, minced	2
2 tbsp	medium curry powder	30 mL
1 tsp	cumin seeds	5 mL
1 lb	skinless boneless chicken, cut into 1-inch (2.5 cm) cubes	500 g
2 cups	chicken broth	500 mL
½ cup	coconut cream (see Tips, left)	125 mL
½ cup	whole raw cashew nuts	125 mL

1. Place drained lentils in a bowl and cover with boiling water. Set aside for 1 hour. Drain thoroughly.

2. In a large skillet or wok, heat oil over low heat. Add onions and cook, stirring occasionally, until softened, about 8 minutes. Add garlic, curry powder and cumin seeds and cook, stirring, until fragrant, about 2 minutes. Add chicken and cook, stirring, until well coated with mixture, about 3 minutes. Stir in broth.

3. Transfer to slow cooker stoneware. Add coconut cream and drained lentils. Cover and cook on Low for 5 hours or on High for $2\frac{1}{2}$ hours, until juices run clear when chicken is pierced with a fork.

4. In a small skillet over medium heat, toast cashews, stirring, until golden, about 3 minutes. Sprinkle over chicken mixture and serve immediately.

Spicy Chicken & Potato Curry

Tips

Serve this curry with hot rice and chutney or pickle.

Depending upon the heat level of your curry powder, this quantity may produce a very spicy curry. If you're heat-averse, use less.

To serve two people: Cut the quantities in half and use a small (approx. 2 quart) slow cooker.

To serve six people: Increase the quantities by half and use a large (approx. 5 quart) slow cooker.

Preparation Time: 10 minutes, pus marinating
Medium (approx. 4 quart) slow cooker
Heat Rating: ♨♨♨

2 lbs	skinless bone-in chicken thighs or drumsticks (about 8)	1 kg
3 tbsp	hot curry powder (see Tips, left)	45 mL
2 tbsp	oil	30 mL
1	onion, halved lengthwise and thinly sliced on the vertical	1
4	cloves garlic, minced	4
2	chicken bouillon cubes, crumbled	2
4	tomatoes, cored and chopped	4
3	potatoes, peeled and diced	3
3	cups coconut milk	750 mL
	Chopped cilantro leaves	

1. Place chicken in a bowl and sprinkle with curry powder. Toss to coat well. Cover and refrigerate for 30 minutes.

2. In a large skillet, heat oil over medium heat. Add onion and garlic and stir-fry until onion is softened, about 3 minutes. Add crumbled bouillon cubes and stir well. Add marinated chicken, with juices, and stir-fry until it begins to brown, about 5 minutes. Add tomatoes and stir-fry, scraping up brown bits from bottom of pan.

3. Transfer to slow cooker stoneware. Add potatoes and coconut milk and stir well. Cover and cook on Low for 6 hours or on High for 3 hours, until juices run clear when chicken is pierced with a fork. Garnish with cilantro and serve immediately.

Chicken Braised in Spiced Yogurt

Serves 4

Tips

Serve with plenty of hot rice.

To purée gingerroot, use a fine, sharp-toothed grater, such as those made by Microplane.

To serve two people: Cut the quantities in half and use a small (approx. 2 quart) slow cooker.

To serve six people: Increase the quantities by half and use a large (approx. 5 quart) slow cooker.

Preparation Time: 20 minutes, plus marinating
Medium (approx. 4 quart) slow cooker
Heat Rating: 🌶🌶

½ cup	plain yogurt (not lower-fat)	125 mL
2 tbsp	oil	30 mL
1 tbsp	liquid honey	15 mL
	Juice of 2 limes	
4 tsp	puréed gingerroot (see Tips, left)	20 mL
6	cloves garlic, minced	6
1 tbsp	sweet paprika	15 mL
1 tbsp	ground coriander	15 mL
2 tsp	ground cumin	10 mL
2 tsp	ground turmeric	10 mL
2 tsp	ground cinnamon	10 mL
2 tsp	dried red chile flakes	10 mL
	Salt and freshly ground black pepper	
2 lbs	skinless bone-in chicken thighs or drumsticks (about 8)	1 kg
¾ cup	water	175 mL

1. In a large bowl, combine yogurt, oil, honey, lime juice, ginger, garlic, paprika, coriander, cumin, turmeric, cinnamon and chile flakes, plus salt and freshly ground pepper to taste. Add chicken and toss until well combined. Cover and refrigerate for at least 6 hours or overnight.

2. Transfer to slow cooker stoneware. Add water. Cover and cook on Low for 6 hours or on High for 3 hours, until juices run clear when chicken is pierced with a fork. Serve immediately.

Spicy Braised Chicken

Serves 6

Tips

Serve this with hot, fluffy rice.

Coconut cream is a thicker, more concentrated version of coconut milk. Look for it in Asian markets. If you can't find it, use the cream that collects on the top of a can of coconut milk after it's been sitting. Do not shake the can before opening.

This produces a very spicy dish. If desired, reduce the quantity of chiles to suit your taste.

Preparation Time: 10 minutes, plus marinating
Medium (approx. 4 quart) slow cooker
Heat Rating: 💧💧💧

Marinade

1 cup	coconut cream (see Tips, left)	250 mL
2	onions, quartered	2
10	green onions, coarsely sliced	10
4	long red chile peppers, coarsely chopped (see Tips, left)	4
3	cloves garlic	3
2 tbsp	coarsely chopped gingerroot	30 mL
1 tbsp	curry powder	15 mL
2 tsp	dried thyme	10 mL
2 tsp	granulated sugar	10 mL
1 tsp	salt	5 mL
3 lbs	skinless bone-in chicken thighs or drumsticks (about 12)	1.5 kg
1¼ cups	chicken broth	300 mL

1. *Marinade:* In a food processor fitted with the metal blade, process coconut cream, onions, green onions, chiles, garlic, ginger, curry powder, thyme, sugar and salt until a smooth paste forms.

2. Transfer to a large bowl and add chicken. Toss until well coated. Cover and refrigerate overnight.

3. Transfer to slow cooker stoneware and add chicken broth. Cover and cook on Low for 6 hours or on High for 3 hours, until juices run clear when chicken is pierced with a fork.

Apple-Spiked Chicken Curry with Eggs

Serves 4

Tips

Serve with mounds of steaming rice.

To hard-cook eggs: Place eggs in a single layer in a saucepan and cover with cold water. Cover and bring to a boil over high heat. Remove from heat and let stand for 10 minutes. Using a slotted spoon, transfer to a bowl of ice water. Cool for about 1 minute before peeling.

Preparation Time: 10 minutes
Medium (approx. 4 quart) slow cooker
Heat Rating:

1 tbsp	freshly squeezed lemon juice	15 mL
2	apples	2
2 tbsp	oil	30 mL
1	onion, chopped	1
2	cloves garlic, minced	2
2 tbsp	curry powder	30 mL
1 tbsp	tomato paste	15 mL
1 cup	coconut milk	250 mL
2 cups	chicken broth	500 mL
12 oz	skinless boneless chicken breast, cut into 1-inch (2.5 cm) cubes	375 g
2 tbsp	cornstarch, dissolved in 2 tbsp (30 mL) cold water	30 mL
4	hard-cooked eggs, peeled and halved lengthwise	4

1. Place lemon juice in a bowl large enough to accommodate the apples and add 1 cup (250 mL) water. Peel, core and coarsely dice the apples, adding to the acidulated water as cut. Set aside.

2. In a skillet, heat oil over medium heat. Add onion and stir-fry until softened, about 3 minutes. Add garlic and curry powder and stir-fry until fragrant, about 2 minutes. Add tomato paste and coconut milk and stir well.

3. Transfer to slow cooker stoneware. Drain reserved apple mixture and add apples to stoneware, discarding soaking water. Add chicken broth and chicken.

4. Cover and cook on Low for 4 hours or on High for 2 hours. Stir in cornstarch mixture. Carefully add eggs, cut side up. Cover and cook on High for 30 minutes, until eggs are heated through and mixture has thickened slightly.

Vietnamese Chicken Rice

Tip

Be sure to use parboiled (converted) rice in the slow cooker. Regular rice tends to become quite sticky.

Preparation Time: 15 minutes
Small (2 to 3½ quart) slow cooker
Heat Rating:

1 cup	long-grain parboiled (converted) white rice	250 mL
1 lb	skinless boneless chicken thighs, diced	500 g
4	shallots, halved and thinly sliced	4
4	cloves garlic, minced	4
1 tsp	minced gingerroot	5 mL
2 cups	boiling chicken broth	500 mL

Garnish

	Small bunch of mint, leaves removed and shredded, stems discarded	
4	green onions, thinly sliced	4

1. In slow cooker stoneware, combine rice, chicken, shallots, garlic and gingerroot. Stir well. Add boiling chicken broth.

2. Cover and cook on Low for 3 hours, until liquid is absorbed and rice fluffs easily with a fork. Spoon into a serving dish and garnish with mint and green onions. Serve immediately.

Jungle Curry with Duck

Serves 4

Tips

This spicy dish originates in Chiang Mai, in the northern part of Thailand.

Prepared jungle curry paste is available online. You will need from 1 to 3 tbsp (15 to 45 mL) for this recipe, depending on how hot you like your curry.

Thai baby eggplants and shrimp paste are available in Asian markets.

Before chopping, remove and discard the tough outer layers of the lemongrass.

Four chile peppers produce a very hot paste. You may want to reduce the quantity of chiles to suit your taste.

Often called Kaffir lime leaves, wild lime leaves are the leaves of a small Asian lime. You can use fresh or frozen varieties. If you can't find them, in this recipe substitute 2 tsp (10 mL) finely grated lime zest.

Shrimp paste, which is made from ground dried fermented shrimp, is available in Asian markets. It lends saltiness and depth of flavor to sauces. If you can't find it, in this recipe substitute 1 anchovy fillet, mashed, or 1 tsp (5 mL) anchovy paste.

Preparation Time: 20 minutes
Medium (approx. 4 quart) slow cooker
Heat Rating: ♨♨♨

Jungle Curry Paste

¼ cup	oil	60 mL
5	Thai shallots, finely chopped	5
6	cloves garlic, chopped	6
3 tbsp	finely chopped cilantro stems	45 mL
2 tbsp	finely chopped lemongrass (see Tips, left)	30 mL
1 tbsp	minced gingerroot	15 mL
4	long green chile peppers, chopped	4
3	wild lime leaves, shredded (see Tips, left)	3
1 tbsp	ground white peppercorns	15 mL
1 tsp	shrimp paste (see Tips, left)	5 mL

Curry

2 tbsp	oil	30 mL
4	bone-in duck legs, skin removed	4
2 cups	chicken broth	500 mL
1 tbsp	fish sauce, such as nam pla	15 mL
½ cup	bamboo shoots, drained and rinsed	125 mL
8 oz	pea (Thai baby) eggplant or 1 small eggplant, trimmed and cut into bite-sized cubes	250 g
	Handful of Thai holy basil leaves, divided	

1. *Jungle Curry Paste:* In a food processor fitted with the metal blade, process oil, shallots, garlic, cilantro, lemongrass, ginger, chiles, lime leaves, white pepper and shrimp paste until a smooth paste forms. (If necessary, add a little water.)

2. *Curry:* In a large skillet, heat oil over high heat. Add curry paste and stir-fry for 2 minutes. Add duck legs and turn until well coated with mixture. Cook for 2 minutes longer.

3. Transfer to slow cooker stoneware. Add broth, fish sauce, bamboo shoots, eggplant and a small handful of the basil leaves. Cover and cook on Low for 6 hours or on High for 3 hours, until duck is very tender. Serve immediately, garnished with remaining basil leaves.

Thai Duck & Bamboo Shoot Curry

Tips

This is delicious served with plenty of hot jasmine rice.

This is a very fiery curry. Unless you are a heat-lover, you might consider reducing the quantity of curry paste to as little as 2 tbsp (30 mL).

Before chopping, remove the tough outer layers of the lemongrass and cut the remaining stalk into several sections. Using the flat side of a knife, smash each piece (this helps to release the flavor).

If you don't like green beans that are well-cooked, use sliced frozen (unthawed) beans in this recipe.

Duck legs are available at good butchers. Usually they turn them into confit, but if you ask, they will set some aside for you.

Preparation Time: 15 minutes
Medium (approx. 4 quart) slow cooker
Heat Rating: ♨♨♨

1 cup	coconut cream, divided	250 mL
¼ cup	Thai red curry paste	60 mL
2 tbsp	oil	30 mL
1 tbsp	soft palm sugar	15 mL
2	stalks lemongrass, smashed and chopped (see Tips, left)	2
4	bone-in duck legs, skin removed (see Tips, left)	4
1	can (14 oz/400 mL) coconut milk	1
1	can (13 oz/400 g) bamboo shoots, drained and rinsed	1
2 cups	sliced green beans (see Tips, left)	500 mL
4	wild lime leaves (see Tips, page 83)	4
3 tbsp	fish sauce, such as nam pla	45 mL
6 tbsp	finely chopped cilantro leaves	90 mL

1. In a large skillet over medium heat, combine ½ cup (125 mL) coconut cream, curry paste and oil. Stir-fry until the oil starts to separate, about 4 minutes. Add sugar and stir-fry for 1 minute. Add lemongrass and duck and turn until duck is well coated with mixture. Cook 2 minutes longer.

2. Transfer to slow cooker stoneware. Add remaining coconut cream, coconut milk, bamboo shoots, green beans, lime leaves and fish sauce and stir well. Cover and cook on Low for 6 hours or on High for 3 hours, until duck is cooked through. Garnish with cilantro and serve immediately.

Green Duck Curry with Carrots & Eggplant

Tips

Serve this curry in warmed bowls over a mound of steamed jasmine rice.

Often called Kaffir lime leaves, wild lime leaves are the leaves of a small Asian lime. You can use fresh or frozen varieties. If you can't find them, in this recipe substitute 1 tbsp (15 mL) finely grated lime zest.

Palm sugar is also known as jaggery. You can substitute raw cane sugar such as Mexican piloncillo, or regular dark brown sugar.

Preparation Time: 10 minutes
Medium (approx. 4 quart) slow cooker
Heat Rating:

1 tbsp	oil	15 mL
3 tbsp	Thai green curry paste	45 mL
2	long green chile peppers, finely chopped	2
4	bone-in duck legs, skin removed	4
1	can (14 oz/400 mL) coconut milk	1
1 cup	chicken broth	250 mL
6	wild lime leaves (see Tips, left)	6
2 tbsp	fish sauce, such as nam pla	30 mL
1 tbsp	soft palm sugar (see Tips, left)	15 mL
8 oz	pea (Thai baby) eggplant or 1 small eggplant, cut into bite-sized cubes	250 g
8 oz	carrots, peeled and cut into bite-sized pieces	250 g
	Large handful of Thai sweet basil leaves	
	Large handful of cilantro leaves	
	Juice of 1 lime	

1. In a large skillet or wok, heat oil over medium-high heat. Add green curry paste and chiles and stir-fry for 3 minutes. Add duck and turn until coated with mixture.

2. Transfer to slow cooker stoneware. Stir in coconut milk, chicken broth, lime leaves, fish sauce, sugar, eggplant and carrots.

3. Cover and cook on Low for 6 hours or on High for 3 hours, until duck is very tender. Stir in basil, cilantro and lime juice and serve immediately.

Fruity Egg & Chicken Curry

Tips

Serve with plenty of hot, fluffy rice.

To hard-cook eggs: Place eggs in a single layer in a saucepan and cover with cold water. Cover and bring to a boil over high heat. Remove from heat and let stand for 10 minutes. Using a slotted spoon, transfer to a bowl of ice water. Cool for about 1 minute before peeling.

Preparation Time: 10 minutes
Medium (approx. 4 quart) slow cooker
Heat Rating:

2 tbsp	oil	30 mL
1	onion, chopped	1
2	cloves garlic, minced	2
2 tbsp	curry powder	30 mL
1 tbsp	tomato paste	15 mL
3 cups	chicken broth, divided	750 mL
12 oz	skinless boneless chicken, cut into bite-size pieces	375 g
2	apples, peeled, cored and roughly chopped	2
1 cup	coconut milk	250 mL
2 tbsp	cornstarch	30 mL
2 tbsp	cold water	30 mL
4	hard-cooked eggs, peeled and halved lengthwise	4

1. In a skillet, heat oil over medium heat. Add onion and stir-fry until softened, about 3 minutes. Add garlic and stir-fry for 1 minute. Add curry powder and stir-fry until fragrant, about 2 minutes. Stir in tomato paste and 1 cup (250 mL) of the broth, scraping up brown bits from bottom of pan.

2. Transfer to slow cooker stoneware. Add chicken, apples, coconut milk and remaining chicken broth. Cover and cook on Low for 4 hours or on High for 2 hours.

3. In a small bowl, combine cornstarch and water. Mix well. Stir into stoneware. Carefully add eggs, cut side up, and spoon a bit of the sauce overtop. Cover and cook on High for 15 minutes, until sauce is slightly thickened and flavors are melded. Serve immediately.

South Indian Egg Curry

Serves 4

Vegetarian Friendly

Tips

Serve with Indian bread and/or basmati rice.

If you prefer a milder curry, reduce the quantity of cayenne.

To hard-cook eggs: Place eggs in a single layer in a saucepan and cover with cold water. Cover and bring to a boil over high heat. Remove from heat and let stand for 10 minutes. Using a slotted spoon, transfer to a bowl of ice water. Cool for about 1 minute before peeling.

Preparation Time: 10 minutes
Medium (approx. 4 quart) slow cooker
Heat Rating: 🌶🌶

2 tbsp	oil	30 mL
1 tbsp	cumin seeds	15 mL
1 tbsp	black mustard seeds	15 mL
1	onion, halved and thinly sliced	1
10	curry leaves	10
2	cloves garlic, minced	2
2	dried red chile peppers	2
1 tsp	cayenne pepper (see Tips, left)	5 mL
1 tbsp	ground coriander	15 mL
½ tsp	ground turmeric	2 mL
2	potatoes, peeled and diced	2
1 cup	canned diced tomatoes, with juice	250 mL
1 tsp	granulated sugar	5 mL
1	can (14 oz/400 mL) coconut milk	1
	Salt	
6	hard-cooked eggs, peeled and cut in half lengthwise (see Tips, left)	6
	Chopped cilantro leaves	

1. In a large skillet, heat oil over medium-high heat. Add cumin and mustard seeds and cover. When the seeds stop popping, reduce heat to medium and add onion. Stir-fry until softened, about 3 minutes. Add curry leaves, garlic and chiles and stir-fry for 1 minute. Add cayenne, coriander and turmeric and stir well. Add potatoes and stir well. Stir in tomatoes and sugar.

2. Transfer to slow cooker stoneware. Stir in coconut milk and season to taste with salt. Cover and cook on Low for 6 hours or on High for 3 hours, until potatoes are tender.

3. Carefully add eggs, cut side up, spooning a little sauce over them. Cover and cook on High for 15 minutes to meld flavors. Garnish with cilantro and serve immediately.

Filipino Egg & Potato Curry

Tips

Serve with rice.

If you are using the outer stalks of celery, peel them first to get rid of the fibrous exterior.

If your curry powder is hot, you may want to reduce the quantity to suit your taste.

To hard-cook eggs: Place eggs in a single layer in a saucepan and cover with cold water. Cover and bring to a boil over high heat. Remove from heat and let stand for 10 minutes. Using a slotted spoon, transfer to a bowl of ice water. Cool for about 1 minute before peeling.

Preparation Time: 15 minutes
Medium (approx. 4 quart) slow cooker
Heat Rating: ♨♨

3 tbsp	oil, divided	45 mL
1	large Spanish onion, cut into 8 wedges	1
3	stalks celery, cut into 1-inch (2.5 cm) lengths	3
3	cloves garlic, minced	3
3 tbsp	curry powder (see Tips, left)	45 mL
4	large potatoes, peeled and diced	4
1 cup	water	250 mL
1	can (14 oz/400 mL) coconut milk	1
1	red bell pepper, seeded and diced	1
4	hard-cooked eggs, peeled and halved lengthwise (see Tips, left)	4
	Salt and freshly ground black pepper	

1. In a large skillet, heat 2 tbsp (30 mL) of the oil over medium-high heat. Add onion and brown lightly on all sides, about 4 minutes. Using a slotted spoon, transfer to slow cooker stoneware as completed. Lower heat to medium.

2. Add remaining oil to pan. Add celery and stir-fry until softened, about 5 minutes. Add garlic and curry powder and stir-fry for 1 minute. Add potatoes and stir-fry for 1 minute. Add water and bring to a boil, stirring and scraping up brown bits from bottom of pan. Pour mixture over onions. Add coconut milk and stir well.

3. Cover and cook on Low for 6 hours or on High for 3 hours, until onion is very tender and potatoes are cooked through.

4. Add bell pepper and stir well. Carefully add eggs, cut side up, and spoon a little of the sauce overtop. Cover and cook on High for 15 minutes, until pepper is tender and flavors are melded. Serve immediately.

Sri Lankan Egg Curry

Serves 4

Vegetarian Friendly

Tips

Serve over hot jasmine rice.

Use a small slow cooker with a capacity of about 2 quarts. Do not try to halve this recipe. To serve 6 people, increase the quantities by half and use a slightly larger (maximum 3 quart) slow cooker, if you wish.

This recipe is fiery. For a less incendiary dish, remove the seeds and membranes of the chiles before mincing. You might also consider reducing the quantity of curry powder.

To hard-cook eggs: Place eggs in a single layer in a saucepan and cover with cold water. Cover and bring to a boil over high heat. Remove from heat and let stand for 10 minutes. Using a slotted spoon, transfer to a bowl of ice water. Cool for about 1 minute before peeling.

Preparation Time: 10 minutes
Small (approx. 2 quart) slow cooker
Heat Rating: ♨♨♨

2 tbsp	oil	30 mL
1	onion, finely chopped	1
10	curry leaves	10
3	cloves garlic, minced	3
1 tbsp	minced gingerroot	15 mL
2	long green chile peppers, minced (see Tips, left)	3
3 tbsp	medium curry powder	45 mL
1	can (14 oz/398 mL) diced tomatoes, with juice	1
	Salt	
6	hard-cooked eggs, peeled and halved lengthwise (see Tips, left)	6
6 tbsp	finely chopped cilantro leaves	90 mL

1. In a skillet, heat oil over medium heat. Add onion, curry leaves, garlic and ginger and stir-fry until onions are softened, about 4 minutes. Add chile peppers and curry powder and stir-fry until fragrant, about 2 minutes. Add tomatoes, with juice, and stir well. Season to taste with salt.

2. Transfer to slow cooker stoneware. Cover and cook on High for 2 hours. Carefully add eggs, cut side up, and spoon a bit of the sauce overtop. Cover and cook on High for 15 minutes, until flavors meld. Garnish with cilantro and serve immediately.

Fish & Shellfish

Madras Fish Curry

Serves 4

Tips

Serve this with steaming hot rice and poppadums.

The best fish to use in this recipe is a firm, oily fish with lots of flavor, such as mackerel, kingfish, bluefish or mahi-mahi.

To serve two people: Cut the quantities in half and use a small (approx. 2 quart) slow cooker.

To serve six people: Increase the quantities by half and use a large (approx. 5 quart) slow cooker.

Preparation Time: 10 minutes
Medium (approx. 4 quart) slow cooker
Heat Rating: ♨♨♨

1 tbsp	oil	15 mL
2 tbsp	Madras curry powder	30 mL
2	red onions, finely chopped	2
¼ cup	finely chopped cilantro leaves	60 mL
1	can (14 oz/400 mL) coconut milk	1
1 lb	skinless fish fillets, cut into 2-inch (5 cm) pieces (see Tips, left)	500 g
	Finely grated zest and juice of 1 lime	

1. In a skillet or wok, heat oil over medium heat. Add curry powder and stir-fry until fragrant, about 2 minutes. Add onions and cilantro and stir-fry for 30 seconds. Stir in coconut milk and transfer to slow cooker stoneware.

2. Add fish and lime zest and juice. Cover and cook on Low for 4 hours or on High for 2 hours, until fish flakes easily when tested with a fork.

Allepy Fish Curry

Serves 4

Tips

Serve this with steamed basmati rice.

Be sure to use tamarind paste (sometimes labeled "concentrate"), which comes in a jar. Tamarind in a block needs to be dissolved in water and pressed through a sieve to remove seeds and pulp before being added to recipes and, therefore, becomes more diluted in flavor and texture.

The best fish to use in this recipe is a firm, oily fish with lots of flavor, such as mackerel, kingfish, bluefish or mahi-mahi.

Preparation Time: 10 minutes, plus soaking
Medium (approx. 4 quart) slow cooker
Heat Rating: ♨♨♨

4	dried red chile peppers	4
1½ cups	loosely packed freshly grated coconut	375 mL
3 tbsp	curry powder	45 mL
1 tbsp	sweet paprika	15 mL
1 cup	coconut milk	250 mL
2 tbsp	tamarind paste (see Tips, left)	30 mL
2	long green chile peppers, halved lengthwise	2
1	piece (1 inch/2.5 cm) peeled gingerroot, grated	1
1	small onion, finely chopped	1
	Salt	
1 lb	skinless fish fillets, cut into 2-inch (5 cm) pieces (see Tips, left)	500 g

1. Soak dried chiles in hot water to cover for 30 minutes, until softened. Drain and discard soaking liquid. Transfer chiles to a food processor fitted with the metal blade. Add coconut, curry powder, paprika and coconut milk and process until a smooth paste forms.

2. Transfer to a skillet. Bring mixture to a gentle simmer over medium-low heat. Add tamarind paste, fresh chiles, ginger and onion. Season with salt to taste. Stir well and simmer for 3 minutes.

3. Place fish in slow cooker stoneware. Add sauce. Cover and cook on Low for 4 hours or on High for 2 hours, until fish flakes easily when tested with a fork. Serve immediately.

White Fish Curry

Serves 4

Tips

Serve this with plenty of steamed rice and Indian pickles, if desired.

If you can't find curry leaves, substitute dried or fresh bay leaves.

For best results, use halibut, turbot or haddock fillets in this recipe.

To serve two people: Cut the quantities in half and use a small (approx. 2 quart) slow cooker.

To serve six people: Increase the quantities by half and use a large (approx. 5 quart) slow cooker.

Preparation Time: 10 minutes, plus soaking
Medium (approx. 4 quart) slow cooker
Heat Rating: ◊

1 tsp	fenugreek seeds	5 mL
¼ cup	warm water	60 mL
1	can (14 oz/400 mL) coconut milk	1
3	onions, finely sliced	3
2	cloves garlic, minced	2
8	curry leaves (see Tips, left)	8
	Salt and freshly ground black pepper	
1 lb	skinless firm white fish fillets, cut into bite-size pieces and patted dry (see Tips, left)	500 g
1 tsp	ground turmeric	5 mL
½ tsp	salt	2 mL
	Freshly squeezed lemon juice	

1. In a small bowl, combine fenugreek seeds and water. Let stand for 30 minutes. Drain, discarding water. Set fenugreek aside.

2. In a saucepan, combine coconut milk, onions, garlic, curry leaves and reserved fenugreek seeds. Season to taste with salt and freshly ground pepper. Bring to a simmer over medium heat. Reduce heat and simmer until onions are softened, about 12 minutes.

3. Sprinkle fish evenly with turmeric and salt. Transfer to slow cooker stoneware. Add coconut milk mixture. Cover and cook on Low for 4 hours or on High for 2 hours, until fish flakes easily when tested with a fork. Add lemon juice to taste. Serve immediately.

Tamarind Fish Curry

Tips

Serve this curry in warmed shallow bowls with steamed basmati rice and poppadums.

Be sure to use tamarind paste (sometimes labeled "concentrate"), which comes in a jar. Tamarind in a block needs to be dissolved in water and pressed through a sieve to remove seeds and pulp before being added to recipes and, therefore, becomes more diluted in flavor and texture.

To purée gingerroot, use a fine, sharp-toothed grater, such as those made by Microplane.

Variation

Substitute another firm white fish such as grouper, haddock or halibut for the cod.

Preparation Time: 15 minutes, plus marinating
Medium (approx. 4 quart) slow cooker
Heat Rating: ♨

1 tbsp	tamarind paste (see Tips, left)	15 mL
¼ cup	rice wine vinegar	60 mL
2 tbsp	cumin seeds	30 mL
1 tsp	ground turmeric	5 mL
1 tsp	cayenne pepper	5 mL
1 tsp	salt	5 mL
1½ lbs	thick cod fillets, cut into bite-size pieces (see Tips, left)	750 g
2 tbsp	oil	30 mL
1	onion, finely chopped	1
2 tbsp	puréed gingerroot (see Tips, left)	30 mL
3	cloves garlic, minced	3
2 tsp	black mustard seeds	10 mL
1	can (28 oz/796 mL) diced tomatoes, with juice	1
1 tsp	granulated sugar	5 mL

1. In a bowl, combine tamarind paste, vinegar, cumin seeds, turmeric, cayenne and salt. Stir well. Add cod and turn to coat evenly. Cover and refrigerate for 30 minutes.

2. Meanwhile, in a skillet or wok, heat oil over high heat. Stir in onion, ginger, garlic and mustard seeds. Reduce heat and cook gently for 10 minutes, stirring occasionally.

3. Add tomatoes and sugar. Stir well and bring to a boil. Reduce heat, cover and simmer, stirring occasionally, for 20 minutes.

4. Transfer to slow cooker stoneware. Add cod, with marinade, and stir gently. Cover and cook on High for 2 hours, until fish flakes easily when tested with a fork.

Fish Mollee

Serves 6 to 8

Tips

Serve this with steamed basmati rice.

If you can't find curry leaves, substitute dried or fresh bay leaves.

Use one large piece of fish to make this mollee, and be aware that the cooking time depends upon the configuration of your fish. The thicker it is, the longer it will take.

Preparation Time: 15 minutes
Medium (approx. 4 quart) slow cooker
Heat Rating: ♨♨

1	onion, quartered	1
½ cup	cilantro leaves	125 mL
4	cloves garlic	4
2	long green chile peppers, quartered	2
1 tbsp	ground cumin	15 mL
1 tsp	ground coriander	5 mL
1 tsp	ground turmeric	5 mL
½ cup	water	125 mL
2 tbsp	oil	30 mL
6	curry leaves	6
1	can (14 oz/400 mL) coconut milk	1
2 lbs	halibut fillet (see Tips, left)	1 kg
	Salt and freshly ground black pepper	
	Cilantro leaves	

1. In a food processor fitted with the metal blade, process onion, cilantro, garlic, chiles, cumin, coriander, turmeric and water until a smooth paste forms. Set aside.

2. In a skillet or wok, heat oil over medium-high heat. Add curry leaves and stir-fry for 30 seconds. Add onion paste and stir-fry until fragrant, about 4 minutes. Remove from heat and stir in coconut milk.

3. Place halibut in slow cooker stoneware. Add onion mixture. Season to taste with salt and freshly ground pepper. Cover and cook on Low for 4 hours or on High for 2 hours, until fish flakes easily when tested with a fork. Garnish with cilantro and serve immediately.

Cochin Fish Curry

Serves 4

Tips

If you don't have freshly grated coconut, substitute unsweetened shredded coconut.

Be sure to use tamarind paste (sometimes labeled "concentrate"), which comes in a jar. Tamarind in a block needs to be dissolved in water and pressed through a sieve to remove seeds and pulp before being added to recipes and, therefore, becomes more diluted in flavor and texture.

A firm white fish such as halibut, haddock or turbot works well in this recipe. If you happen to be making this curry in India, look for pomfret, which is also known as butterfish in that country.

Preparation Time: 10 minutes
Medium (approx. 4 quart) slow cooker
Heat Rating: ♦

2 tbsp	freshly grated coconut (see Tips, left)	30 mL
1 tsp	turmeric	5 mL
½ tsp	cayenne pepper	2 mL
2 tbsp	oil	30 mL
1 tsp	mustard seeds	5 mL
20	curry leaves	20
2	onions, thinly sliced	2
4	long green chile peppers, sliced	4
1	piece (1 inch/2.5 cm) peeled gingerroot, cut into matchsticks	1
6	cloves garlic, finely chopped	6
1	can (14 oz/400 mL) coconut milk	1
1 tbsp	tamarind paste (see Tips, left)	15 mL
1½ lbs	skinless firm white fish fillets, cut into 1-inch (2.5 cm) pieces (see Tips, left)	750 mL

1. In a small bowl, combine coconut, turmeric and cayenne. Set aside.

2. In a skillet or wok, heat oil over medium-high heat. Add mustard seeds and cover. When the seeds stop popping, uncover, reduce heat to medium and add curry leaves. Stir well. Add onion, chiles, ginger and garlic and stir-fry until very fragrant and onion begins to color, about 5 minutes. Add turmeric mixture and stir-fry for 2 minutes.

3. Transfer to slow cooker stoneware. Add coconut milk and tamarind paste and stir well. Add fish and stir gently. Cover and cook on Low for 4 hours or on High for 2 hours, until fish flakes easily when tested with a fork. Serve immediately.

Hot & Sour Thai Fish Curry

Serves 6

Tips

Serve this curry in warmed shallow bowls or soup plates with plenty of Thai jasmine rice.

This curry is fiery. For a less incendiary dish, reduce the number of chile peppers to suit your taste.

Before chopping or smashing the lemongrass, remove and discard the tough outer layers. If smashing, cut the remaining stalk into several sections and, using the flat side of a knife, crush each piece (this helps to release the flavor).

Palm sugar is also known as jaggery. You can substitute raw cane sugar such as Mexican piloncillo, or regular dark brown sugar.

Shrimp paste, which is made from ground dried fermented shrimp, is available in Asian markets. It lends saltiness and depth of flavor to sauces. If you can't find it, in this recipe substitute half an anchovy fillet, mashed, or ¹/₂ tsp (2 mL) anchovy paste.

Preparation Time: 10 minutes
Medium (approx. 4 quart) slow cooker
Heat Rating: 🌶🌶🌶

2 tbsp	chopped lemongrass (see Tips, left)	30 mL
5	dried red chile peppers (see Tips, left)	5
2	cloves garlic	2
1 tbsp	fish sauce, such as nam pla	15 mL
1 tsp	salt	5 mL
1 tsp	ground turmeric	5 mL
1 tsp	soft palm sugar (see Tips, left)	5 mL
¹/₂ tsp	shrimp paste (see Tips, left)	2 mL
2	stalks lemongrass, smashed (see Tips, left)	2
2 tbsp	freshly squeezed lemon juice	30 mL
1 tbsp	tamarind paste (see Tips, page 97)	15 mL
2 cups	water, divided	500 mL
1 cup	cubed (¹/₂ inch/1 cm) pineapple	250 mL
6	skinless salmon fillets, each about 5 oz (150 g)	6

1. In a blender or small food processor, process chopped lemongrass, chiles, garlic, fish sauce, salt, turmeric, sugar and shrimp paste until smoothly blended. (You may need to add a little water.)

2. Transfer to slow cooker stoneware. In a small bowl, combine lemon juice, tamarind paste and ¹/₂ cup (125 mL) of the water. Mix well. Add to stoneware along with smashed lemongrass, pineapple and remaining water and stir well. Add salmon fillets. Cover and cook on Low for 4 hours or on High for 2 hours, until fish flakes easily when tested with a fork. Serve immediately.

Sindhi Beef Curry (page 13)

Cambodian Pork & Lemongrass
Curry (page 23)

Bombay Chicken Curry (page 48)

Butter Chicken (page 50)

Thai Green Chicken
Curry (page 63)

Bombay Aloo (page 126)

Goan Xacutti Curry (page 128)

Tomato-Based Vegetable Curry (page 137)

Beet Curry (page 132)

Spiced Chickpea Curry (page 172)

Channa Masala (page 174)

Chile & Tomato Chutney (page 180)

Sri Lankan Fish Curry

Tips

Serve this with hot jasmine rice — white or brown, to suit your preference.

If you can't find curry leaves, substitute dried or fresh bay leaves.

Be sure to use tamarind paste (sometimes labeled "concentrate"), which comes in a jar. Tamarind in a block needs to be dissolved in water and pressed through a sieve to remove seeds and pulp before being added to recipes and, therefore, becomes more diluted in flavor and texture.

Preparation Time: 10 minutes
Medium (approx. 4 quart) slow cooker
Heat Rating: 🌶🌶

2 tbsp	oil	30 mL
1	large onion, chopped	1
4	cloves garlic, finely chopped	4
10	curry leaves (see Tips, left)	10
2 tbsp	medium curry powder	30 mL
1 tsp	ground turmeric	5 mL
1 tbsp	tamarind paste (see Tips, left)	15 mL
2	tomatoes, coarsely chopped	2
1	can (14 oz/400 mL) coconut milk	1
1¾ lbs	skinless firm white fish fillets, cut into 1-inch (2.5 cm) pieces	875 g
	Salt	

1. In a skillet or wok, heat oil over medium heat. Add onion, garlic and curry leaves and stir-fry until onion is lightly golden, about 8 minutes. Sprinkle curry powder and turmeric over mixture and stir-fry until fragrant, about 2 minutes. Stir in tamarind paste and tomatoes, with juices.

2. Transfer to slow cooker stoneware and stir in coconut milk. Add fish and stir gently. Season to taste with salt. Cover and cook on Low for 4 hours or on High for 2 hours, until fish flakes easily when tested with a fork. Serve immediately.

Vietnamese Fish Curry

Tips

Serve with steamed rice.

To purée gingerroot, use a fine, sharp-toothed grater, such as those made by Microplane.

Often called Kaffir lime leaves, wild lime leaves are the leaves of a small Asian lime. You can use fresh or frozen varieties. If you can't find them, in this recipe substitute 1 tbsp (15 mL) finely grated lime zest.

Preparation Time: 15 minutes
Medium (approx. 4 quart) slow cooker
Heat Rating: 🔥🔥🔥

1 tbsp	oil	15 mL
4	shallots, finely chopped	4
4	cloves garlic, minced	4
2 tbsp	finely chopped lemongrass	30 mL
1 tbsp	puréed gingerroot (see Tips, left)	15 mL
1 tbsp	curry powder	15 mL
1 tsp	ground cinnamon	5 mL
6	whole star anise	6
1	can (14 oz/400 mL) coconut milk	1
13 oz	salmon fillet, skin removed, cut into bite-sized pieces	400 g
10 oz	jumbo shrimp (21 to 25), peeled and deveined	300 g
6	wild lime leaves (see Tips, left)	6
6	green onions, finely chopped	6
20	Thai sweet basil leaves, chopped	20
¼ cup	finely chopped cilantro leaves	60 mL

1. In a skillet or wok, heat oil over medium-high heat. Add shallots, garlic, lemongrass and ginger and stir-fry for 4 minutes. Add curry powder, cinnamon and star anise and stir-fry until very fragrant, about 2 minutes. Stir in coconut milk.

2. Transfer to slow cooker stoneware. Add salmon, shrimp and lime leaves. Cover and cook on High for 2 hours, until salmon flakes easily when tested with a fork and shrimp are pink and opaque. Stir in green onions, basil and cilantro and serve immediately.

Balinese Yellow Fish Curry with Potatoes

Serves 6

Tips

Serve with steamed rice.

To serve three people: Cut the quantities in half and use a small (approx. 2 quart) slow cooker.

To serve nine people: Increase the quantities by half and use a large (approx. 5 quart) slow cooker.

Variation

Substitute halibut for the cod.

Preparation Time: 15 minutes
Medium (approx. 4 quart) slow cooker
Heat Rating: ♨♨

1	onion, chopped	1
3	cloves garlic, chopped	3
1	piece (½ inch/1 cm) peeled gingerroot	1
2	long green chile peppers, quartered	2
1 tbsp	ground turmeric	15 mL
2 tbsp	oil	30 mL
1 cup	coconut milk	250 mL
1 cup	water	250 mL
2	potatoes, peeled and diced	2
2	tomatoes, coarsely chopped	2
	Salt	
1¾ lbs	thick cod fillets, skin removed, cut into 1-inch (2.5 cm) cubes	875 g
	Chopped cilantro leaves	

1. In a food processor fitted with the metal blade, process onion, garlic, ginger, chiles and turmeric until onion is very finely chopped and mixture is blended.

2. In a large skillet or wok, heat oil over medium heat. Add onion paste and stir-fry until fragrant, about 5 minutes. Stir in coconut milk and water.

3. Transfer to slow cooker stoneware. Add potatoes and tomatoes. Season to taste with salt. Cover and cook High for 3 hours, until potatoes are tender and mixture is bubbling. Stir in cod. Cover and cook on High until fish flakes easily when tested with a fork, about 10 minutes. Serve immediately, garnished with cilantro leaves.

Seychelles Monkfish Curry

Serves 6

Tips

Serve with rice.

To purée gingerroot, use a fine, sharp-toothed grater, such as those made by Microplane.

Be sure to use tamarind paste (sometimes labeled "concentrate"), which comes in a jar. Tamarind in a block needs to be dissolved in water and pressed through a sieve to remove seeds and pulp before being added to recipes and, therefore, becomes more diluted in flavor and texture.

Preparation Time: 10 minutes
Medium (approx. 4 quart) slow cooker
Heat Rating: ♨♨

2 tbsp	oil	30 mL
2	onions, finely chopped	2
2 tbsp	curry powder	30 mL
1 tsp	ground turmeric	5 mL
2	cloves garlic, minced	2
1 tsp	puréed gingerroot (see Tips, left)	5 mL
½ tsp	tamarind paste (see Tips, left)	2 mL
2 lbs	monkfish tail, skin removed, cut into bite-size pieces	1 kg
2 cups	fish broth	500 mL
1 tbsp	fresh thyme leaves	15 mL
1	star anise	1

1. In a skillet or wok, heat oil over low heat. Add onions and stir-fry until lightly golden, about 10 minutes. Add curry powder and turmeric and stir-fry for 1 minute, until fragrant. Add garlic, ginger and tamarind paste and stir well.

2. Transfer to slow cooker stoneware. Add monkfish, broth, thyme and star anise. Cover and cook on High for 2½ to 3 hours, until fish is cooked through. Serve immediately.

Halibut & Tomato Curry

I loved this it -
Dick didn't -
used
salmon

Serves 6

Tip

Serve this in warmed shallow bowls over a layer of basmati rice or, for something a little different, rice noodles.

Variations

Substitute cod, turbot or haddock fillets for the halibut.

Preparation Time: 15 minutes, plus marinating
Medium (approx. 4 quart) slow cooker
Heat Rating: ♨♨

¼ cup	freshly squeezed lemon juice	60 mL
¼ cup	rice wine vinegar	60 mL
2 tbsp	cumin seeds	30 mL
2 tbsp	curry powder	30 mL
1 tsp	salt	5 mL
1¾ lbs	thick halibut fillets, skin removed, cut into 1-inch (2.5 cm) cubes	875 g
1 tbsp	oil	15 mL
1	onion, finely chopped	1
3	cloves garlic, finely chopped	3
1 tbsp	minced gingerroot	15 mL
1	can (14 oz/398 mL) diced tomatoes, with juice	1
1 tsp	granulated sugar	5 mL

1. In a shallow dish, combine lemon juice, vinegar, cumin seeds, curry powder and salt. Add halibut and turn to coat evenly. Cover and refrigerate for 30 minutes.

2. When halibut has finished marinating, in a skillet or wok, heat oil over medium heat. Add onion and stir-fry until softened, about 3 minutes. Add garlic and ginger and stir-fry for 1 minute. Add tomatoes, with juice, and sugar and stir well.

3. Transfer to slow cooker stoneware. Add halibut, with marinade. Cover and cook on High for 2 hours, until fish flakes easily when tested with a fork. Serve immediately.

Steamed Banana-Leaf Fish

Tips

Accompany these fish packets with plenty of hot rice.

If you don't have fresh coconut, use frozen coconut, thawed.

If you prefer a milder result, reduce the quantity of chile peppers.

Preparation Time: 30 minutes
Medium (approx. 4 quart) slow cooker
Heat Rating: 🔥🔥🔥

4	banana leaves, thawed if frozen	4
1½ cups	loosely packed freshly grated coconut	375 mL
1 cup	loosely packed cilantro leaves	250 mL
½ cup	loosely packed mint leaves	125 mL
4	long green chile peppers, chopped (see Tips, left)	4
5	cloves garlic, minced	5
1 tsp	puréed gingerroot (see Tip, page 103)	5 mL
2 tsp	ground cumin	10 mL
2 tsp	ground coriander	10 mL
1½ tsp	brown sugar	7 mL
3 tbsp	oil, divided	45 mL
	Salt	
4	thick skinless cod fillets, each about 7 oz (200 g)	4
	Juice of 2 limes	

1. Cut each banana leaf into a 9½-inch (24 cm) square. Place in a pan of very hot water until softened, about 10 seconds. Wipe dry with paper towels and set aside.

2. In a food processor fitted with the metal blade (you can also use a blender or mortar and pestle), process coconut, cilantro, mint, chiles, garlic, ginger, cumin, coriander and brown sugar until a smooth paste forms. Set aside.

3. In a small skillet, heat 1 tbsp (15 mL) oil over low heat. Add coconut paste and cook, stirring, until fragrant, about 3 minutes. Season to taste with salt. Remove from heat and set aside.

Tip

To purée gingerroot, use a fine, sharp-toothed grater, such as those made by Microplane.

4. Arrange one banana-leaf square on a work surface. Place one piece of fish in the center of the square and brush both sides of the fish liberally with one-quarter of the coconut paste. Drizzle with one-quarter of the lime juice and one-quarter of the remaining oil. Fold over the edges of the banana leaf like a parcel and secure with a bamboo skewer or string. Repeat with remaining banana leaves, fish, coconut paste, lime juice and oil.

5. Place packets in slow cooker stoneware, overlapping slightly if necessary. Cover and cook on High for 2 to 3 hours or until the fish flakes easily when tested with a fork.

Spicy Braised Halibut

Tips

Serve with steamed rice.

Adjust the quantity of cayenne pepper to suit your preference. If you prefer a milder sauce, use less.

Depending upon the configuration of your slow cooker, you may need a bit more (or less) sliced lemon to cover the bottom.

Variation

Substitute cod fillets for the halibut.

Preparation Time: 10 minutes
Medium (approx. 4 quart) slow cooker
Heat Rating:

1 cup	packed cilantro leaves	250 mL
3 tbsp	extra virgin olive oil	45 mL
3 tbsp	white wine vinegar	45 mL
4	cloves garlic, coarsely chopped	4
1 tsp	ground cumin	5 mL
1 tsp	ground paprika	5 mL
1 tsp	cayenne pepper (see Tips, left)	5 mL
2 (approx.)	lemons, thinly sliced (see Tips, left)	2
4	thick halibut fillets, each about 7 oz (210 g)	4
	Salt	

1. In a food processor fitted with the metal blade (or in a blender), process cilantro, olive oil, vinegar, garlic, cumin, paprika and cayenne until smoothly blended. Set aside.

2. Arrange lemon slices in a single layer over the bottom of the stoneware, overlapping as necessary. Place fish on top in a single layer. Season to taste with salt. Spoon cilantro mixture evenly over the fish. Cover and cook on High for 2 to 3 hours, until fish flakes easily when tested with a fork. Serve immediately.

Thai Fish Ball Curry

Tips

Serve with hot jasmine rice.

Before chopping the lemongrass, remove and discard the tough outer layers.

Palm sugar is also known as jaggery. You can substitute raw cane sugar such as Mexican piloncillo, or regular dark brown sugar.

Often called Kaffir lime leaves, wild lime leaves are the leaves of a small Asian lime. You can use fresh or frozen varieties. If you can't find them, in this recipe substitute 2 tsp (10 mL) finely grated lime zest.

Cooked fish balls are available in well-stocked Asian markets, especially those specializing in Thai foods.

Preparation Time: 10 minutes
Medium (approx. 4 quart) slow cooker
Heat Rating: 🌶🌶

1 tbsp	oil	15 mL
1 tbsp	Thai red curry paste	15 mL
1	carrot, diced	1
1 tbsp	minced lemongrass (see Tips, left)	15 mL
2 cups	coconut milk	500 mL
2 tsp	soft palm sugar (see Tips, left)	10 mL
4	wild lime leaves (see Tips, left)	4
2 tsp	fish sauce, such as nam pla	10 mL
1 lb	cooked fish balls (see Tips, left)	500 g
6 oz	sugar snap peas, halved	175 g
	Thinly sliced red chile peppers	
	Cilantro leaves	

1. In a skillet or wok, heat oil over medium heat. Add curry paste and stir-fry for 2 minutes. Add carrot and lemongrass and stir-fry for 2 minutes. Add coconut milk and stir well.

2. Transfer to slow cooker stoneware. Add palm sugar, lime leaves and fish sauce and stir well. Add fish balls. Cover and cook on High for 2 hours, until hot and bubbly. Stir in peas. Cover and cook on High for 10 minutes, until peas are tender. Serve in warmed bowls, garnished with sliced chile pepper and cilantro leaves.

Lobster Curry

Tips

Serve with hot rice.

If you prefer a milder curry, reduce the quantity of curry powder.

Preparation Time: 5 minutes
Medium (approx. 4 quart) slow cooker
Heat Rating:

2 tbsp	butter or ghee	10 mL
1	onion, finely chopped	1
2	cloves garlic, minced	2
2 tbsp	curry powder	30 mL
2	green onions (white and green parts), thinly sliced	2
2	large tomatoes, finely chopped	2
1 cup	cold water	250 mL
2 tsp	cornstarch, dissolved in 2 tbsp (30 mL) cold water	10 mL
2 lbs	cooked lobster meat, coarsely chopped	1 kg

1. In a skillet or wok, melt butter over medium heat. Add onion, garlic, curry powder, green onions and tomatoes and stir-fry for 6 minutes. Add water and bring to a boil, stirring and scraping up brown bits from bottom of pan.

2. Transfer to slow cooker stoneware. Cover and cook on Low for 4 hours or on High for 2 hours. Add cornstarch mixture and lobster meat. Cover and cook on High for 20 minutes, until sauce has thickened and flavors are melded.

Scallop & Spinach Curry

Serves 4

Tips

Serve this curry over plenty of steaming rice.

To serve two people: Cut the quantities in half and use a small (approx. 2 quart) slow cooker.

To serve six people: Increase the quantities by half and use a large (approx. 5 quart) slow cooker.

Preparation Time: 5 minutes
Medium (approx. 4 quart) slow cooker
Heat Rating: ♨♨

2 tbsp	oil	30 mL
2 tsp	black mustard seeds	10 mL
1 tbsp	curry powder	15 mL
4	cloves garlic, minced	4
2 tsp	minced gingerroot	10 mL
½ tsp	granulated sugar	2 mL
1	can (14 oz/398 mL) diced tomatoes, with juice	1
1 lb	large sea scallops	500 g
8 oz	baby spinach leaves, coarsely chopped	250 g
¼ cup	heavy or whipping (35%) cream	60 mL
	Salt and freshly ground black pepper	

1. In a skillet or wok, heat oil over medium-high heat. Add mustard seeds and cover. When the seeds stop popping (in a minute or two), uncover, reduce heat to medium and stir in curry powder, garlic, ginger and sugar. Add tomatoes and stir well.

2. Transfer to slow cooker stoneware and add scallops. Cover and cook on Low for 4 hours or on High for 2 hours. Stir in spinach and cream. Cover and cook on High for 15 minutes, until spinach is wilted and scallops are opaque throughout. Season to taste with salt and pepper and serve immediately.

Malaysian Scallop Curry

Serves 6

Tips

Before chopping the lemongrass, remove and discard the tough outer layers.

Palm sugar is also known as jaggery. You can substitute raw cane sugar such as Mexican piloncillo, or regular dark brown sugar.

If you prefer a milder curry, reduce the quantity of cayenne pepper.

Shrimp paste, which is made from ground dried fermented shrimp, is available in Asian markets. It lends saltiness and depth of flavor to sauces. If you can't find it, in this recipe substitute half an anchovy fillet, mashed, or $\frac{1}{2}$ tsp (2 mL) anchovy paste.

Preparation Time: 15 minutes
Medium (approx. 4 quart) slow cooker
Heat Rating: 👐

2 cups	coconut milk	500 mL
8	small shallots, coarsely chopped	8
$\frac{1}{2}$ cup	coarsely chopped lemongrass (see Tips, left)	125 mL
2 tbsp	raw skinless peanuts	30 mL
1 tbsp	soft palm sugar (see Tips, left)	15 mL
2 tsp	minced gingerroot	10 mL
2 tsp	ground cumin	10 mL
1 tsp	ground coriander	5 mL
1 tsp	cayenne pepper (see Tips, left)	5 mL
$\frac{1}{2}$ tsp	shrimp paste (see Tips, left)	2 mL
7 oz	sugar snap peas, trimmed	210 g
1$\frac{3}{4}$ lbs	large sea scallops	875 g
	Thai sweet basil leaves	
	Chopped roasted peanuts	
	Finely sliced long red or Thai bird's-eye chile peppers	

1. In a food processor fitted with the metal blade, process coconut milk, shallots, lemongrass, raw peanuts, palm sugar, gingerroot, cumin, coriander, cayenne and shrimp paste until smooth.

2. Transfer to slow cooker stoneware. Add peas and scallops. Cover and cook on Low for 4 hours or on High for 2 hours, until scallops are opaque. Serve immediately, garnished with basil leaves, roasted peanuts and red chiles.

Kerala Crab Curry

Serves 4

Tips

Serve with plenty of steaming hot rice.

If you prefer a milder curry, reduce the quantity of cayenne pepper.

For convenience, use a can of pasteurized crabmeat. Look for it in the refrigerated section of your fish market.

If you can't find curry leaves, substitute dried or fresh bay leaves.

Preparation Time: 15 minutes
Medium (approx. 4 quart) slow cooker
Heat Rating:

1	can (14 oz/400 mL) coconut milk	1
3	onions, finely chopped	3
6	cloves garlic, minced	6
1 tbsp	minced gingerroot	15 mL
10	curry leaves (see Tips, left)	10
1	piece (4 inches/10 cm) cinnamon stick	1
1 tsp	ground turmeric	5 mL
1 tsp	cayenne pepper (see Tips, left)	5 mL
2 cups	cooked crabmeat (see Tips, left)	500 mL
	Salt and freshly ground black pepper	

1. In slow cooker stoneware, combine coconut milk, onions, garlic, ginger, curry leaves, cinnamon stick, turmeric and cayenne. Stir well. Cover and cook on High for 2 hours, until mixture is bubbling.

2. Stir in crabmeat and season to taste with salt and freshly ground black pepper. Cover and cook on High for 15 minutes, until crab is heated through and flavors are melded. Serve immediately.

Shrimp & Mango Curry

Tips

If you prefer a milder curry, reduce the quantity of cayenne pepper.

Palm sugar is also known as jaggery. You can substitute raw cane sugar such as Mexican piloncillo, or regular dark brown sugar.

If you're using canned coconut milk, be sure to shake well before using. The cream layer collects on the top after it's been sitting.

Be sure to use tamarind paste (sometimes labeled "concentrate"), which comes in a jar. Tamarind in a block needs to be dissolved in water and pressed through a sieve to remove seeds and pulp before being added to recipes and, therefore, becomes more diluted in flavor and texture.

Preparation Time: 15 minutes
Medium (approx. 4 quart) slow cooker
Heat Rating: 🌶🌶

4	cloves garlic, minced	4
1 tbsp	minced gingerroot	15 mL
2 tbsp	ground coriander	30 mL
1 tbsp	sweet paprika	15 mL
2 tsp	ground cumin	10 mL
1 tsp	salt	5 mL
1 tsp	cayenne pepper (see Tips, left)	5 mL
½ tsp	ground turmeric	2 mL
1 tbsp	soft palm sugar (see Tips, left)	15 mL
1	can (14 oz/400 mL) coconut milk	1
1 tbsp	tamarind paste (see Tips, left)	15 mL
1	mango, peeled, pitted and sliced	1
1 lb	jumbo shrimp (21 to 25), peeled and deveined	500 g
	Finely chopped cilantro leaves	

1. In slow cooker stoneware, mix together garlic, ginger, coriander, paprika, cumin, salt, cayenne, turmeric and sugar. Add coconut milk and tamarind paste and mix well.

2. Add mango and shrimp. Cover and cook on High for 2 hours, until shrimp are pink and opaque. Serve immediately, garnished with cilantro.

Bangkok Shrimp Curry with Pineapple

Serves 4

Tips

Serve this with Thai jasmine rice.

Be sure to remove the tough outer layers of the lemongrass stalk before chopping. Otherwise your dish will be quite fibrous.

Often called Kaffir lime leaves, wild lime leaves are the leaves of a small Asian lime. You can use fresh or frozen varieties. If you can't find them, in this recipe substitute 1½ tsp (7 mL) finely grated lime zest.

Palm sugar is also known as jaggery. You can substitute raw cane sugar such as Mexican piloncillo, or regular dark brown sugar.

Preparation Time: 15 minutes
Medium (approx. 4 quart) slow cooker
Heat Rating: ♨♨♨

½	onion, coarsely chopped	½
2 tbsp	finely chopped lemongrass (see Tips, left)	30 mL
2	long red chile peppers, thinly sliced	2
1 tbsp	minced gingerroot	15 mL
4	cloves garlic, crushed	4
1 tsp	ground turmeric	5 mL
1 tsp	ground coriander	5 mL
3	wild lime leaves, shredded (see Tips, left)	3
1 tbsp	soft palm sugar (see Tips, left)	15 mL
1 tbsp	fish sauce, such as nam pla	15 mL
1	can (14 oz/400 mL) coconut milk	1
1 lb	jumbo shrimp (21 to 25), peeled and deveined	500 g
1 cup	cubed (¾ inch/2 cm) pineapple	250 mL
3½ oz	cherry tomatoes	105 g
6 tbsp	coarsely chopped cilantro leaves	90 mL

1. In a food processor fitted with the metal blade, process onion, lemongrass, chiles, ginger, garlic, turmeric, coriander, lime leaves, sugar, fish sauce and coconut milk until a smooth paste forms.

2. Transfer to slow cooker stoneware. Add shrimp, pineapple and cherry tomatoes. Cover and cook on High for 2 hours, until shrimp are pink and opaque. Stir in cilantro and serve immediately.

Spicy Shrimp Curry with Eggplant and Pineapple

Serves 4

Tip

As noted, this recipe is fiery. For a less incendiary dish, reduce the quantity of curry paste. You might also consider reducing the quantity of fresh chile peppers.

Preparation time: 5 minutes
Medium (approx. 4 quart) slow cooker
Heat Rating: ♨♨♨

¼ cup	oil, divided	60 mL
1	Asian eggplant, cut into bite-size cubes	1
1 tbsp	Thai green curry paste (see Tips, left)	15 mL
1	can (14 oz/400 mL) coconut milk	1
10 oz	pineapple, cubed	300 g
3 tbsp	pineapple juice	45 mL
2 to 3	long green chile peppers (see Tips, left)	2 to 3
1¾ lbs	jumbo shrimp (21 to 25), deveined, shells left on	875 g
1 tbsp	fish sauce, such as nam pla	15 mL

1. In a large skillet or wok, heat 2 tbsp (30 mL) of the oil over medium heat. Add eggplant and stir-fry until lightly browned, about 6 minutes. Transfer to slow cooker stoneware. Add remaining oil and curry paste and stir-fry until fragrant, about 4 minutes. Stir in coconut milk.

2. Transfer to slow cooker stoneware. Add pineapple, pineapple juice, whole green chiles and shrimp. Cover and cook on High for 2 hours, until sauce is hot and bubbly and shrimp are pink and opaque. Season with fish sauce and serve immediately.

Masala Fennel Shrimp

Tips

Serve with plenty of steamed rice.

If you can't find curry leaves, substitute dried or fresh bay leaves.

To serve three people: Cut the quantities in half and use a small (approx. 2 quart) slow cooker.

To serve nine people: Increase the quantities by half and use a large (approx. 5 quart) slow cooker.

Preparation Time: 15 minutes
Medium (approx. 4 quart) slow cooker
Heat Rating: 🔥🔥

1 tbsp	oil	15 mL
12	curry leaves	12
2	large shallots, halved and sliced finely	2
1 tbsp	minced garlic	15 mL
2 tsp	minced gingerroot	10 mL
1 tbsp	curry powder	15 mL
1 tbsp	fennel seeds	15 mL
5	large ripe tomatoes, chopped	5
1½ lbs	jumbo shrimp (21 to 25), peeled and deveined	750 g
	Salt	

1. In a large wok or skillet, heat oil over medium heat. Add curry leaves and stir-fry for 30 seconds. Add shallots and stir-fry for 4 minutes, until softened. Add garlic, ginger, curry powder and fennel seeds and stir-fry for 30 seconds. Add tomatoes, with juices, and stir well.

2. Transfer to slow cooker stoneware. Cover and cook on Low for 4 hours or on High for 2 hours, until bubbling. Add shrimp. Cover and cook on High for 15 minutes or until shrimp are pink and opaque. Season to taste with salt and serve immediately.

Spicy Shrimp

Tips

Serve this with plenty of hot rice.

To serve two people: Cut the quantities in half and use a small (approx. 2 quart) slow cooker.

To serve six people: Increase the quantities by half and use a large (approx. 5 quart) slow cooker.

Preparation Time: 10 minutes, plus marinating
Medium (approx. 4 quart) slow cooker
Heat Rating: ♨♨

1¼ lb	jumbo shrimp (21 to 25), peeled and deveined	625 g
3 tbsp	freshly squeezed lime juice	45 mL
1 tsp	salt	5 mL
1 tbsp	oil	15 mL
1	small onion, finely chopped	1
2	cloves garlic, minced	2
2 tsp	minced gingerroot	10 mL
1 tsp	cayenne pepper	5 mL
1 tsp	sweet paprika	5 mL
2 tsp	tomato paste	10 mL
1 tsp	granulated sugar	5 mL
	Chopped cilantro leaves	

1. In a bowl, combine shrimp, lime juice and salt. Toss well. Cover and refrigerate for 30 minutes. Drain, reserving liquid. Transfer shrimp to slow cooker stoneware.

2. In a skillet or wok, heat oil over low heat. Add onion, garlic and ginger and cook, stirring occasionally, until softened and beginning to color, about 12 minutes. Stir in cayenne, paprika, tomato paste, sugar and reserved marinating liquid. Scrape over shrimp and season to taste with salt.

3. Cover and cook on High for 2 hours, until shrimp are pink and opaque. Serve immediately, garnished with cilantro.

Coconut Shrimp Curry

Tips

Serve this with hot, fluffy rice.

If you have access to ajwain, an Indian spice that is similar to thyme, by all means use it in this recipe.

Preparation Time: 10 minutes
Medium (approx. 4 quart) slow cooker
Heat Rating: ♨♨♨

2 tbsp	oil	30 mL
1	onion, finely chopped	1
2	cloves garlic, minced	2
2	long red chile peppers, minced	2
1 tbsp	mild curry powder	15 mL
1 tsp	dried thyme or ajwain (see Tips, left)	5 mL
1 cup	canned diced tomatoes, with juice	250 mL
1 lb	jumbo shrimp (21 to 25), peeled and deveined	500 g
1	can (14 oz/400 mL) coconut milk	1
	Salt and freshly ground black pepper	
1	red bell pepper, seeded and diced	1
6	green onions (white and green parts), thinly sliced	6

1. In a skillet or wok, heat oil over medium heat. Add onion and stir-fry until softened, about 3 minutes. Add garlic, chiles, curry powder and thyme and stir-fry until fragrant, about 2 minutes. Add tomatoes, with juice, and bring to a boil, stirring and scraping up any brown bits from bottom of pan.

2. Transfer to slow cooker stoneware. Add shrimp and coconut milk and season to taste with salt and freshly ground pepper. Cover and cook on High for 2 hours, until shrimp are pink and opaque. Add bell pepper and green onions. Cover and cook on High for 15 minutes, until pepper is tender. Serve immediately.

Chettinad Pepper Shrimp

Tips

Serve this with rice.

As noted, this recipe is fiery. For a less incendiary dish, reduce the number of dried chile peppers to suit your taste.

Preparation Time: 15 minutes
Medium (approx. 4 quart) slow cooker
Heat Rating: 🔥🔥🔥

2 tbsp	oil	30 mL
3	dried red chile peppers, crumbled (see Tips, left)	3
1 tsp	cracked black peppercorns	5 mL
1 tsp	crushed fennel seeds or star anise	5 mL
10	small shallots, finely chopped	10
4	cloves garlic, minced	4
2 tbsp	tomato paste	30 mL
	Salt	
1 cup	water	250 mL
1¾ lbs	jumbo shrimp (21 to 25), peeled and deveined	875 g
2 tbsp	green peppercorns in brine, drained	30 mL

1. In a skillet or wok, heat oil over medium heat. Add chiles, black peppercorns and fennel seeds and stir-fry until fragrant, about 2 minutes. Increase heat to high. Add shallots, garlic and tomato paste. Season with salt. Add water and stir well.

2. Transfer to slow cooker stoneware. Add shrimp, cover and cook on High for 2 hours, until shrimp are pink and opaque. Stir in green peppercorns and serve immediately.

Spicy Cilantro Shrimp

Tips

Serve with steamed white rice and Indian-style pickles.

Shrimp powder is ground dried shrimp. It is available in Asian or Latin American markets.

To purée garlic, use a fine, sharp-toothed grater, such as those made by Microplane.

Preparation Time: 10 minutes
Medium (approx. 4 quart) slow cooker
Heat Rating: ♨♨

1 lb	jumbo shrimp (21 to 25), peeled and deveined	500 g
¼ cup	rice flour	60 mL
1 tbsp	medium curry powder	15 mL
1 tsp	shrimp powder (see Tips, left)	5 mL
2	shallots, grated	2
4	cloves garlic, puréed (see Tips, left)	4
¼ cup	finely chopped cilantro leaves	60 mL
1	can (14 oz/400 mL) coconut milk	1
	Salt and freshly ground black pepper	

1. Using a sharp knife, slit the shrimp lengthwise and place in slow cooker stoneware.

2. In a bowl, combine rice flour, curry powder, shrimp powder, shallots, garlic, cilantro and coconut milk. Stir well and season to taste with salt and freshly ground pepper. Pour over shrimp and stir well.

3. Cover and cook on High for 2 hours, until shrimp are pink and opaque.

Achari Shrimp

Tips

To purée garlic and gingerroot use a fine, sharp-toothed grater, such as those made by Microplane.

If you can't find curry leaves, substitute dried or fresh bay leaves.

To serve three people: Cut the quantities in half and use a small (approx. 2 quart) slow cooker.

To serve nine people: Increase the quantities by half and use a large (approx. 5 quart) slow cooker.

Preparation Time: 20 minutes
Medium (approx. 4 quart) slow cooker
Heat Rating: 🌶🌶

2 tbsp	oil	30 mL
8	shallots, finely chopped	8
8	curry leaves	8
1 tbsp	puréed garlic (see Tips, left)	15 mL
1 tbsp	puréed gingerroot	15 mL
3	long red chile peppers, halved lengthwise	3
1 tbsp	ground coriander	15 mL
2 tsp	cumin seeds	10 mL
2 tsp	black mustard seeds	10 mL
2 tsp	nigella seeds	10 mL
2 tsp	fennel seeds	10 mL
	Salt and freshly ground black pepper	
1	can (14 oz/398 mL) diced tomatoes, with juice	1
1¾ lbs	jumbo shrimp (21 to 25), peeled and deveined	875 g
6 tbsp	finely chopped cilantro leaves	90 mL

1. In a skillet or wok, heat oil over medium heat. Add shallots and stir-fry until lightly golden, about 10 minutes. Add curry leaves, garlic, ginger and chile peppers and stir-fry for 1 minute. Add ground coriander and cumin, mustard, nigella and fennel seeds. Season to taste with salt and freshly ground pepper and stir-fry until fragrant, about 2 minutes. Stir in tomatoes, with juice.

2. Transfer to slow cooker stoneware. Add shrimp. Cover and cook on High for 2 hours, until shrimp are pink and opaque. Stir in cilantro and serve immediately.

Malabari Spiced Shrimp

Serves 4

Tips

As noted, this recipe is fiery. For a less incendiary dish, reduce the cayenne pepper to $\frac{1}{4}$ to $\frac{1}{2}$ tsp (1 to 2 mL). You might also consider using only half a fresh chile pepper.

Be sure to use tamarind paste (sometimes labeled "concentrate"), which comes in a jar. Tamarind in a block needs to be dissolved in water and pressed through a sieve to remove seeds and pulp before being added to recipes and, therefore, becomes more diluted in flavor and texture.

To purée gingerroot, use a fine, sharp-toothed grater, such as those made by Microplane.

Preparation Time: 15 minutes
Medium (approx. 4 quart) slow cooker
Heat Rating: ♨♨♨

1 tbsp	curry powder	15 mL
2 tsp	ground cumin	10 mL
1 tsp	tamarind paste (see Tips, left)	5 mL
1 tsp	ground turmeric	5 mL
1 tsp	cayenne pepper (see Tips, left)	5 mL
$\frac{1}{2}$ cup	water, divided	125 mL
1 lb	jumbo shrimp (21 to 25), peeled and deveined	500 g
3	cloves garlic, minced	3
1 tsp	puréed gingerroot (see Tips, left)	5 mL
1	long red chile pepper, sliced thinly	1
$\frac{1}{2}$ cup	coconut milk	125 mL
	Salt	
6 tbsp	finely chopped cilantro leaves	90 mL

1. In a bowl, combine curry powder, cumin, tamarind paste, turmeric and cayenne. Add $\frac{1}{4}$ cup (60 mL) of the water and mix well. Set aside.

2. In slow cooker stoneware, combine shrimp, garlic, ginger and chile pepper. Toss to coat. Add curry powder mixture, coconut milk and remaining $\frac{1}{4}$ cup (60 mL) water and stir well.

3. Cover and cook on High for 2 hours, until shrimp are pink and opaque. Season to taste with salt and stir in cilantro. Serve immediately.

Aromatic Shrimp Pilaf

Tip

Be sure to use parboiled (also known as converted) rice. Because the process of parboiling keeps the kernels from sticking together, it works best in the slow cooker.

Preparation Time: 10 minutes
Medium (approx. 4 quart) slow cooker
Heat Rating: ♨♨

2 tbsp	oil	30 mL
1	large onion, finely chopped	1
2	cloves garlic, minced	2
1 tbsp	curry powder	15 mL
1 cup	long-grain parboiled (converted) white rice, preferably basmati	250 mL
2 cups	boiling water	500 mL
	Finely grated zest and juice of 1 large lime	
	Salt and freshly ground black pepper	
10 oz	peeled, deveined, cooked shrimp	300 g
1/4 cup	finely chopped cilantro leaves	60 mL

1. In a skillet or wok, heat oil over medium heat. Add onion and stir-fry until softened, about 3 minutes. Add garlic and stir-fry for 1 minute. Add curry powder and stir-fry until fragrant, about 1 minute. Add rice and stir well.

2. Transfer to slow cooker stoneware. Add boiling water and lime zest. Season to taste with salt and freshly ground black pepper.

3. Cover and cook on Low for 3 hours, until liquid is absorbed and rice fluffs easily with a fork. Stir in lime juice, shrimp and cilantro. Cover and cook on High until shrimp are heated through and flavors are melded, about 10 minutes. Serve immediately.

Thai-Style Mussel Curry

Preparation Time: 15 minutes
Medium (approx. 4 quart) slow cooker
Heat Rating: 🌶🌶🌶

Serves 4

Tips

Serve this in warmed large bowls.

Before cutting the lemongrass, remove the tough outer layers and discard.

Before cleaning the mussels, sort through them and discard any that are cracked or have broken shells. The mussels should be tightly closed or they should close when tapped lightly on the work surface. Discard any that do not close.

1 tbsp	oil	15 mL
6	cloves garlic, minced	6
1 tbsp	minced gingerroot	15 mL
1 tsp	Thai green curry paste	5 mL
6	green onions, finely chopped	6
3 to 4	long red chile peppers, split in half lengthwise	3 to 4
1	can (14 oz/400 mL) coconut milk	1
2	stalks lemongrass, trimmed and halved lengthwise (see Tips, left)	2
	Finely grated zest and juice of 2 limes	
3 tbsp	soy sauce	45 mL
1 tsp	granulated sugar	5 mL
3 lbs	mussels, cleaned (see Tips, page 122)	1.5 kg
½ cup	chopped cilantro leaves	125 mL
	Salt and freshly ground pepper	

1. In a skillet or wok, heat oil over medium-high heat. Add garlic, ginger, curry paste, green onions and chiles and stir-fry for 30 seconds. Remove from heat and stir in coconut milk.

2. Transfer to slow cooker stoneware. Add lemongrass, lime zest and juice, soy sauce, sugar and mussels. Cover and cook on High for 2 hours, until mixture is bubbling and mussels have opened. Remove and discard any that do not open. Stir in cilantro and season to taste with salt and freshly ground pepper.

Spicy Mussel Curry

Serves 4

Tips

Serve this in warmed large bowls accompanied by lemon wedges for squeezing.

If you have access to ajwain, an Indian spice that is similar to thyme, by all means use it in this recipe.

Before cleaning the mussels, sort through them and discard any that are cracked or have broken shells. The mussels should be tightly closed or they should close when tapped lightly on the work surface. Discard any that do not close.

If you are using farmed mussels (which is likely) they will only need to be thoroughly rinsed under water before use in this recipe. If the mussels are not farmed, they will need to be carefully scrubbed with a wire brush under cold running water. Any fibrous beard (only on mussels that are not farmed) should be trimmed off with a sharp knife.

Preparation Time: 15 minutes
Medium (approx. 4 quart) slow cooker
Heat Rating: 🌶🌶🌶

6	green onions, trimmed and coarsely chopped	6
2	cloves garlic, coarsely chopped	2
2	long red chile peppers, coarsely chopped	2
1 tbsp	curry powder	15 mL
1 tsp	dried thyme or ajwain (see Tips, left)	5 mL
	Finely grated zest and juice of 1 lime	
3 tbsp	oil	45 mL
1 cup	diced tomatoes, with juice	250 mL
3 lbs	mussels, cleaned (see Tips, left)	1.5 kg
	Lemon wedges	

1. In a food processor fitted with the metal blade, process onions, garlic, chiles, curry powder, thyme, lime zest and juice and oil until a rough paste forms. If necessary, add a bit more oil.

2. In a skillet or wok over medium-high heat, stir-fry curry paste until fragrant, about 2 minutes. Add tomatoes and stir well.

3. Transfer to slow cooker stoneware and add mussels. Cover and cook on High for 2 hours, until mixture is bubbling and mussels have opened. Remove and discard any that have not opened. Serve immediately with lemon wedges for squeezing over.

Spiced Coconut Mussel Curry

Serves 4

Tips

If you are heat-averse, remove the seeds and membranes after slitting the chile pepper. You might also consider reducing the quantity of curry powder.

If you're using canned coconut milk, be sure to shake well before using. The cream layer collects on top after it's been sitting.

Use freshly grated coconut or frozen grated coconut, thawed.

Before cleaning the mussels, sort through them and discard any that are cracked or have broken shells. The mussels should be tightly closed or they should close when tapped lightly on the work surface. Discard any that do not close.

If you are using farmed mussels (which is likely) they will only need to be thoroughly rinsed under water before use in this recipe. If the mussels are not farmed, they will need to be carefully scrubbed with a wire brush under cold running water. Any fibrous beard (on mussels that are not farmed) should be trimmed off with a sharp knife.

Preparation Time: 15 minutes
Medium (approx. 4 quart) slow cooker
Heat Rating: 🔥🔥🔥

2 tbsp	oil	30 mL
2	shallots, very finely chopped	2
2	cloves garlic, minced	2
1	long red chile pepper, slit lengthwise) (see Tips, left	1
1	piece (1½ inches/3.5 cm) peeled gingerroot, cut into shreds	1
1 tbsp	curry powder	15 mL
2	plum tomatoes, diced	2
1 cup	coconut milk	250 mL
3 lbs	mussels, cleaned (see Tips, left) Large handful of chopped cilantro leaves	1.5 kg
3 tbsp	grated coconut (see Tips, left)	45 mL

1. In a skillet or wok, heat oil over medium heat. Add shallots, garlic, chile pepper and ginger and stir-fry for 4 minutes, until shallots are very soft. Stir in curry powder. Add tomatoes and coconut milk and stir well.

2. Transfer to slow cooker stoneware and add mussels. Cover and cook on High for 2 hours, until mixture is bubbling and mussels have opened. Remove and discard any that have not opened. Stir in cilantro. Serve immediately, garnished with coconut.

Vegetables, Fruits & Nuts

❀❀❀

Bombay Aloo

Tips

Because potatoes cook very slowly in the slow cooker, it is important to cut them into small pieces to ensure they will be tender in the appropriate time frame.

Potatoes oxidize quickly on contact with air, so after they are diced, submerge them in a bowl of cold water to prevent browning. Drain before adding to the pan.

Preparation Time: 5 minutes
Medium (approx. 4 quart) slow cooker
Heat Rating: ♨♨

2 tbsp	oil	30 mL
2 tsp	black mustard seeds	10 mL
10	curry leaves	10
2 tsp	ground cumin	10 mL
2 tsp	ground coriander	10 mL
1 tsp	ground turmeric	5 mL
½ tsp	cayenne pepper	2 mL
1 lb	potatoes, peeled and diced (see Tips, left)	500 g
1 cup	water	250 mL
	Salt and freshly ground black pepper	
6 tbsp	chopped cilantro leaves	90 mL
	Lemon wedge	

1. In a large skillet or wok, heat oil over medium-high heat. Add mustard seeds and cover. When the seeds stop popping, uncover, reduce heat to medium and add curry leaves, cumin, coriander, turmeric and cayenne. Stir-fry until fragrant, about 1 minute. Add potatoes and stir-fry for 3 minutes. Add water and bring to a boil, scraping up brown bits from bottom of pan. Season to taste with salt and freshly ground pepper.

2. Transfer to slow cooker stoneware. Cover and cook on Low for 6 hours or on High for 3 hours, until potatoes are tender. Stir in cilantro and squeeze lemon juice to taste overtop. Serve immediately.

Cumin Potato Curry

Serves 4

Vegan Friendly

Tips

Because potatoes cook very slowly in the slow cooker, it is important to cut them into small pieces to ensure they will be tender in the appropriate time frame.

Potatoes oxidize quickly on contact with air, so after they are diced, submerge them in a bowl of cold water to prevent browning. Drain before adding to the pan.

Preparation Time: 20 minutes
Medium (approx. 4 quart) slow cooker
Heat Rating: ⚬

2 tbsp	oil	30 mL
1 tsp	black mustard seeds	5 mL
1 tbsp	cumin seeds	15 mL
10	curry leaves	10
2 tsp	ground cumin	10 mL
2 tsp	ground coriander	10 mL
1 tsp	ground turmeric	5 mL
1 lb	potatoes, peeled and diced (see Tips, left)	500 g
	Salt and freshly ground black pepper	
1 cup	boiling water	250 mL
¼ cup	chopped cilantro leaves	60 mL
	Juice of 1 lime	

1. In a large skillet or wok, heat oil over medium-high heat. Add mustard seeds and cover. When the seeds stop popping, uncover, reduce heat to medium and add cumin seeds, curry leaves, ground cumin, coriander and turmeric. Stir-fry until fragrant, about 1 minute. Add potatoes and stir-fry for 3 minutes. Season to taste with salt and freshly ground black pepper. Add boiling water and return to a boil, scraping up brown bits from the bottom of pan.

2. Transfer to slow cooker stoneware. Cover and cook on Low for 6 hours or on High for 3 hours, until potatoes are tender. Stir in cilantro and sprinkle lime juice over top. Serve immediately.

Goan Xacutti Curry

Tips

In Indian cooking, white poppy seeds are used to thicken sauces. If you can't find them, substitute white sesame seeds.

To toast coconut, place in a dry skillet and stir-fry over medium-low heat until golden brown.

Preparation Time: 15 minutes
Medium (approx. 4 quart) slow cooker
Heat Rating: ♨♨♨

Curry Paste

1 tbsp	oil	15 mL
2	pieces (each about 2 inches/5 cm) cinnamon stick	2
2 tsp	white poppy seeds (see Tips, left)	10 mL
2 tsp	whole black peppercorns	10 mL
4	dried red chile peppers	4
3	whole cloves	3
2	onions, coarsely chopped	2
4	cloves garlic, coarsely chopped	4
1 cup	toasted desiccated coconut (see Tips, left)	250 mL
3	potatoes, peeled and cut into ½-inch (1 cm) cubes	3
2	large carrots, peeled and cut into ½-inch (1 cm) cubes	2
1	can (14 oz/398 mL) diced tomatoes, with juice	1
1 cup	boiling water	250 mL
	Salt	
1 cup	sweet green peas, thawed if frozen	250 mL

1. *Curry Paste:* In a small skillet, heat oil over medium heat. Add cinnamon, poppy seeds, peppercorns, chiles and cloves and stir-fry until very fragrant, about 2 minutes. Transfer to a blender or food processor fitted with the metal blade. Add onions, garlic and toasted coconut and process until a smooth paste forms (add a little water if necessary). Set aside.

2. Place potatoes and carrots in slow cooker stoneware. Add tomatoes, with juice, boiling water and reserved curry paste. Stir well and season to taste with salt.

3. Cover and cook on Low for 6 hours or on High for 3 hours, until potatoes are tender. Stir in peas. Cover and cook on High for 15 minutes, until peas are tender. Serve immediately.

Mushroom & Tomato Curry

Tips

To serve two people: Cut the quantities in half and use a small (approx. 2 quart) slow cooker.

To serve six people: Increase the quantities by half and use a large (approx. 5 quart) slow cooker.

Preparation Time: 15 minutes
Medium (approx. 4 quart) slow cooker
Heat Rating:

1	onion, chopped	1
4	cloves garlic, chopped	4
1 tbsp	chopped peeled gingerroot	15 mL
1 tbsp	curry powder	15 mL
3 tbsp	water	45 mL
¼ cup	oil, divided	60 mL
1 lb	large white mushrooms, halved or thickly sliced	500 g
4	tomatoes, finely chopped	4
½ cup	coconut milk	125 mL
	Salt and freshly ground black pepper	
6 tbsp	finely chopped cilantro leaves	90 mL

1. In a food processor fitted with the metal blade, process onion, garlic, ginger, curry powder and water until smoothly blended. Set aside.

2. In a large skillet or wok, heat 2 tbsp (30 mL) of the oil over high heat. Add mushrooms and stir-fry for 5 minutes. Transfer to slow cooker stoneware and wipe skillet clean. Lower heat to medium.

3. Heat remaining oil in skillet. Add onion mixture and stir-fry for 4 minutes. Stir in tomatoes and coconut milk. Season to taste with salt and freshly ground pepper. Cover and cook on Low for 6 hours or on High for 3 hours, until mushrooms are tender. Stir in cilantro and serve immediately.

Sweet Potato Curry

Serves 4

Vegan Friendly

Tip

To purée gingerroot use a fine, sharp-toothed grater, such as those made by Microplane.

Preparation Time: 10 minutes
Medium (approx. 4 quart) slow cooker
Heat Rating: 🌶🌶

1	onion, finely chopped	1
3	cloves garlic, minced	3
2	long red chile peppers, minced	2
1 tsp	ground turmeric	5 mL
1 tsp	puréed gingerroot (see Tip, left)	5 mL
1 cup	coconut milk	250 mL
1 tbsp	soy sauce	15 mL
1 tbsp	freshly squeezed lemon juice	15 mL
1 lb	sweet potatoes, peeled and cut into ¾-inch (2 cm) cubes	500 g
1 cup	boiling water	250 mL
¼ cup	chopped cilantro leaves	60 mL

1. In slow cooker stoneware combine onion, garlic, chiles, turmeric, ginger, coconut milk, soy sauce and lemon juice. Add sweet potatoes and boiling water. Cover and cook on High for 3 hours, until sweet potatoes are tender. Stir in cilantro and serve immediately.

Butternut Squash Curry

Serves 4

Vegan Friendly

Tips

Serve with hot jasmine rice.

Be sure to shake the can of coconut milk well before using, as the cream layer collects on the top after it's been sitting.

Preparation Time: 10 minutes
Medium (approx. 4 quart) slow cooker
Heat Rating: 🌶🌶

	Finely grated zest and juice of 1 lime	
1 tbsp	Thai green curry paste	15 mL
1 tbsp	soy sauce	15 mL
1	can (14 oz/400 mL) coconut milk, divided	1
1	large butternut squash, peeled, seeded and cut into ¾-inch (2 cm) cubes	1

1. In a small bowl, combine lime zest and juice, curry paste and soy sauce. Stir in a bit of coconut milk to blend. Add to slow cooker stoneware along with remaining coconut milk. Stir in squash.

2. Cover and cook on High for 3 hours, until squash is tender. Serve immediately.

Thai Red Curry with Pumpkin

Tips

As noted, this recipe is fiery. For a less incendiary dish, reduce the curry paste to suit your taste. One tbsp (15 mL) produces a pleasantly spicy dish.

Often called Kaffir lime leaves, wild lime leaves are the leaves of a small Asian lime. You can use fresh or frozen varieties. If you can't find them, in this recipe substitute 1 tbsp (15 mL) finely grated lime zest.

Palm sugar is also known as jaggery. You can substitute raw cane sugar such as Mexican piloncillo, or regular dark brown sugar.

Variation

Substitute butternut or acorn squash for the pumpkin.

Preparation Time: 20 minutes
Medium (approx. 4 quart) slow cooker
Heat Rating: ♨♨♨

2 tbsp	oil	30 mL
1	red onion, thinly sliced on the vertical	1
2	cloves garlic, minced	2
1 tsp	puréed gingerroot (see Tip, page 130)	5 mL
3 tbsp	Thai red curry paste (see Tips, left)	45 mL
1	can (14 oz/400 mL) coconut milk	1
5 cups	cubed (1 inch/2.5 cm) peeled pumpkin (see Variation, below)	1.25 L
1 cup	boiling water	250 mL
6	wild lime leaves (see Tips, left)	6
2 tsp	soft palm sugar	10 mL
3	stalks lemongrass, smashed	3
	Salt and freshly ground black pepper	
	Small handful of Thai sweet basil leaves	
1/3 cup	coarsely chopped roasted peanuts	75 mL

1. In a large skillet or wok, heat oil over medium heat. Add onion, garlic and ginger and stir-fry for 3 minutes, until onion is softened. Add curry paste and stir-fry for 3 minutes. Stir in coconut milk.

2. Transfer to slow cooker stoneware. Add pumpkin, boiling water, lime leaves, palm sugar and lemongrass. Cover and cook on Low for 6 hours or on High for 3 hours, until pumpkin is tender. Season to taste with salt and freshly ground pepper. Garnish with basil and peanuts and serve immediately.

Beet Curry

Tips

If you can't find curry leaves, substitute dried or fresh bay leaves.

You can use fresh tomatoes or canned diced tomatoes. You will need about half of a 14-oz (398 mL) can for this recipe.

Coconut cream is a thicker, more concentrated version of coconut milk. Look for it in Asian markets. If you can't find it, skim off the top layer of a can of coconut milk that has been left standing (not shaken).

Preparation Time: 15 minutes
Medium (approx. 4 quart) slow cooker
Heat Rating: ♦♦

2 tbsp	oil	30 mL
1 tsp	black mustard seeds	5 mL
1	onion, chopped	1
2	cloves garlic, minced	2
2	long red chile peppers, finely chopped	2
8	curry leaves (see Tips, left)	8
1 tsp	ground turmeric	5 mL
1 tsp	cumin seeds	5 mL
1	piece (2 inches/5 cm) cinnamon stick	1
1 lb	beets, peeled and cut into matchsticks	500 g
1 cup	diced tomatoes, with juice (see Tips, left)	250 mL
1 cup	water	250 mL
	Salt	
¼ cup	coconut cream (see Tips, left)	60 mL
	Juice of 1 lime	
	Chopped cilantro leaves	

1. In a large skillet or wok, heat oil over medium-high heat. Add mustard seeds and cover. When the seeds stop popping, uncover, reduce heat to medium and add onion, garlic and chiles. Stir-fry until onion is soft and translucent, about 5 minutes. Add curry leaves, turmeric, cumin, cinnamon and beets and stir-fry for 2 minutes.

2. Transfer to slow cooker stoneware. Add tomatoes, water and salt to taste. Cover and cook on Low for 6 hours or on High for 3 hours, until beets are tender. Stir in coconut cream and lime juice. Garnish with cilantro and serve immediately.

Cauliflower Curry

Serves 4

Vegan Friendly

Tips

To purée garlic, use a fine, sharp-toothed grater, such as those made by Microplane.

Use 1 package (10 oz/300 g) frozen cauliflower florets for this quantity.

To serve two people: Cut the quantities in half and use a small (approx. 2 quart) slow cooker.

To serve six people: Increase the quantities by half and use a large (approx. 5 quart) slow cooker.

Preparation Time: 10 minutes
Medium (approx. 4 quart) slow cooker
Heat Rating: ♨

2 tbsp	oil	30 mL
8	green onions, white and green parts, cut into 2-inch (5 cm) lengths	8
2 tbsp	curry powder	30 mL
2 tsp	puréed garlic (see Tip, left)	10 mL
2 tsp	ground ginger	10 mL
2 cups	cauliflower florets (see Tips, left)	500 mL
1	can (14 oz/398 mL) diced tomatoes, with juice	1
1 cup	cooked chickpeas (see Tips, left)	250 mL
	Salt and freshly ground black pepper	
1	red bell pepper, seeded and cut into bite-size cubes	1
1	green bell pepper, seeded and cut into bite-size cubes	1
¼ cup	plain yogurt	60 mL
	Large handful of chopped mint leaves	

1. In a large skillet or wok, heat oil over medium heat. Add green onions and stir-fry for 3 minutes. Add curry powder, garlic and ginger and stir-fry until fragrant, about 1 minute. Add cauliflower and stir-fry for 3 minutes. Stir in tomatoes, with juice.

2. Transfer to slow cooker stoneware. Add chickpeas and season to taste with salt and freshly ground black pepper. Cover and cook on Low for 6 hours or on High for 3 hours, until cauliflower is tender. Add red and green bell peppers and stir well. Cover and cook on High for 10 minutes, until peppers are tender and flavors are melded. Drizzle with yogurt, garnish with mint and serve immediately.

Zucchini Curry

Tip

Serve with plenty of steamed basmati rice.

Preparation Time: 5 minutes
Medium (approx. 4 quart) slow cooker
Heat Rating: 🌶🌶

2 tbsp	oil	30 mL
1	large onion, finely chopped	1
4	large zucchini, cut into ½-inch (1 cm) cubes	4
2	cloves garlic, minced	2
½ tsp	cayenne pepper	2 mL
¼ tsp	ground turmeric	1 mL
1	can (28 oz/796 mL) tomatoes, with juice	1
1 tsp	dried mint	5 mL
	Salt and freshly ground black pepper	

1. In a large skillet or wok, heat oil over medium heat. Add onion and stir-fry until soft, about 3 minutes. Add zucchini and stir-fry for 5 minutes. Add garlic, cayenne and turmeric and stir well. Stir in tomatoes, scraping up any brown bits from bottom of pan.

2. Transfer to slow cooker stoneware. Add mint. Cover and cook on Low for 6 hours or on High for 3 hours. Season to taste with salt and freshly ground pepper and serve immediately.

Shredded Cabbage Curry

Tip

Use freshly grated or dried coconut. To toast coconut, place in a dry skillet and stir-fry over medium-low heat until golden brown.

Preparation Time: 10 minutes
Medium (approx. 4 quart) slow cooker
Heat Rating: 🌶🌶

3 cups	finely shredded cabbage	750 mL
1	onion, finely chopped	1
2	long green chile peppers, minced	2
1 tsp	black mustard seeds	5 mL
½ tsp	ground turmeric	2 mL
1¼ cups	boiling water	300 mL
⅓ cup	shredded coconut, lightly toasted (see Tips, left)	75 mL

1. In slow cooker stoneware, combine cabbage, onion, chiles, mustard seeds, turmeric and boiling water. Stir well. Cover and cook on High for 3 hours, until cabbage is tender. Garnish with toasted coconut and serve immediately.

Ceylonese Pea Curry

Tips

Serve with steamed white rice.

If you can't find curry leaves, substitute dried or fresh bay leaves.

Remove the tough outer layers of the lemongrass and cut the remaining stalk into several sections. Using the flat side of the knife, smash each piece (this helps to release the flavor).

Preparation time: 10 minutes, plus soaking
Medium (approx. 4 quart) slow cooker
Heat Rating: ♨♨

2½ cups	raw cashew nuts (10 oz/300 g), soaked in cold water for 3 hours	625 mL
	Salt	
1 tsp	ground turmeric	5 mL
2 tbsp	oil	30 mL
2	onions, thinly sliced on the vertical	2
6	curry leaves (see Tips, left)	6
2	cloves garlic, minced	2
1	piece (2 inches/5 cm) cinnamon stick	1
1 tbsp	medium curry powder	15 mL
1 tsp	cayenne pepper	5 mL
1 tsp	sweet paprika	5 mL
1¼ cups	coconut milk	300 mL
1	stalk lemongrass, smashed (see Tips, left)	1
1 cup	sweet green peas, thawed if frozen	250 mL
¼ cup	chopped cilantro leaves	60 mL

1. Drain cashews and discard soaking liquid. Place in a saucepan and add cold water to cover. Season lightly with salt and sprinkle with turmeric. Bring to a boil, reduce heat and simmer until soft and creamy, about 30 minutes. Drain, discarding cooking liquid. Transfer cashews to slow cooker stoneware.

2. Meanwhile, in a skillet or wok, heat oil over medium heat. Add onions and stir-fry for 5 minutes. Add curry leaves, garlic and cinnamon and stir-fry for 3 minutes. Add curry powder, cayenne and paprika and stir-fry until fragrant, about 1 minute. Stir in coconut milk.

3. Transfer to slow cooker stoneware and add lemongrass. Season to taste with salt. Cover and cook on High for 3 hours. Stir in peas. Cover and cook on High for 15 minutes, until peas are tender. Sprinkle with cilantro and serve immediately.

Sri Lankan Green Bean Curry

Serves 4
Vegan Friendly

Tips

If you can't find curry leaves, substitute dried or fresh bay leaves.

To serve two people: Cut the quantities in half and use a small (approx. 2 quart) slow cooker.

To serve six people: Increase the quantities by half and use a large (approx. 5 quart) slow cooker.

Preparation Time: 10 minutes
Medium (approx. 4 quart) slow cooker
Heat Rating: 🌢🌢

1 tbsp	oil	15 mL
1	onion, sliced	1
2	long green chile peppers, sliced	2
1	clove garlic, minced	1
6	curry leaves (see Tips, left)	6
1 tbsp	curry powder	15 mL
½ tsp	fenugreek seeds	2 mL
¼ tsp	ground turmeric	1 mL
1 lb	green beans, trimmed and cut in half crosswise	500 g
½ cup	coconut milk	125 mL
	Salt and freshly ground black pepper	
	Squeeze of fresh lime juice	

1. In a skillet or wok, heat oil over medium heat. Add onion and stir-fry for 3 minutes, until softened. Add chiles, garlic and curry leaves and stir-fry for 5 minutes, until onions begin to brown. Add curry powder, fenugreek and turmeric and stir-fry until fragrant, about 2 minutes.

2. Transfer to slow cooker stoneware. Add beans and coconut milk and season to taste with salt and freshly ground black pepper. Stir well. Cover and cook on Low for 3 to 4 hours or until beans are very tender. Add a squeeze of lime juice and serve immediately.

Tomato-Based Vegetable Curry

Tips

Because potatoes cook very slowly in the slow cooker, it is important to cut them into small pieces to ensure they will be tender in the appropriate time frame.

Potatoes oxidize quickly on contact with air, so after they are diced, submerge them in a bowl of cold water to prevent browning. Drain before adding to the pan.

Serve with plenty of rice.

Preparation Time: 15 minutes
Medium (approx. 4 quart) slow cooker
Heat Rating: 🌶🌶🌶

1 tbsp	oil	15 mL
2	onions, finely chopped	2
3	cloves garlic, minced	3
2	long red chile peppers, minced	2
2 tsp	curry powder	10 mL
1 tsp	dried thyme	5 mL
1 lb	potatoes, peeled and diced (see Tips, left)	500 g
1¼ cups	vegetable broth or water	300 mL
2	carrots, peeled and sliced	2
1	can (14 oz/398 mL) diced tomatoes, with juice	1
2	zucchini, halved lengthwise and sliced	2
1	red bell pepper, seeded and diced	1
6	green onions, including green parts, finely chopped	6
	Salt and freshly ground black pepper	

1. In a large skillet or wok, heat oil over medium-high heat. Add onions and stir-fry until softened, about 3 minutes. Add garlic, chiles, curry powder and thyme and stir-fry for 1 minute. Add potatoes and stir-fry for 3 minutes. Add vegetable broth and bring to a boil, scraping up brown bits from bottom of pan.

2. Transfer to slow cooker stoneware. Add carrots and tomatoes, with juice, and stir well. Cover and cook on Low for 5 hours or on High for 2½ hours. Add zucchini, bell pepper and green onions. Cover and cook on High for 30 minutes, until vegetables are tender and flavors are melded. Season to taste with salt and freshly ground pepper and serve immediately.

South Indian Vegetable Curry

<table>
<tr><td>Serves 4</td></tr>
<tr><td>Vegan Friendly</td></tr>
</table>

Tips

To purée gingerroot, use a fine, sharp-toothed grater, such as those made by Microplane.

If you can't find curry leaves, substitute dried or fresh bay leaves.

Because potatoes cook very slowly in the slow cooker, it is important to cut them into small pieces to ensure they will be tender in the appropriate time frame.

Potatoes oxidize quickly on contact with air, so after the potato is diced, submerge it in a bowl of cold water to prevent browning. Drain before adding to the pan.

Preparation Time: 15 minutes
Medium (approx. 4 quart) slow cooker
Heat Rating: ♨♨

2 tbsp	oil	30 mL
2 tsp	black mustard seeds	10 mL
6	shallots, thinly sliced on the vertical	6
10	curry leaves	10
1	long green chile pepper, thinly sliced	1
2 tsp	puréed gingerroot (see Tips, left)	10 mL
2 tsp	ground cumin	10 mL
1 tsp	ground turmeric	5 mL
6	black peppercorns	6
1	large potato, peeled and diced	1
⅓ cup	vegetable broth or water	125 mL
2	carrots, peeled and sliced	2
1	zucchini, sliced	1
1 cup	coconut milk	250 mL
	Salt and freshly ground black pepper	
	Juice of ½ lemon	

1. In a large skillet or wok, heat oil over medium-high heat. Add mustard seeds and cover. When the seeds stop popping, uncover, reduce heat to medium and add shallots, curry leaves, chile, ginger, cumin, turmeric and peppercorns. Stir-fry for 2 minutes, until fragrant. Add potato and stir-fry for 3 minutes. Add vegetable broth and bring to a boil, scraping up brown bits from bottom of pan.

2. Transfer to slow cooker stoneware. Add carrots, zucchini and coconut milk. Cover and cook on Low for 6 hours or on High for 3 hours, until vegetables are tender. Season to taste with salt and freshly ground pepper and sprinkle with lemon juice. Serve immediately.

Cambodian Vegetable Curry

Tips

Remove the tough outer layers of the lemongrass and cut the remaining stalk into several sections. Using the flat side of the knife, smash each piece. (This helps to release the flavor.)

Look for dry-style tofu in Asian markets. If you can't find it, use extra-firm tofu, but before using, press the water out of it. Wrap in several layers of paper towels and weigh down with a foil-wrapped brick. Let stand for 30 minutes.

Preparation Time: 15 minutes
Medium (approx. 4 quart) slow cooker
Heat Rating: ♨♨

1 tbsp	oil	15 mL
6	shallots, coarsely chopped	6
1	clove garlic, minced	1
1	piece (1½ inches/4 cm) gingerroot, peeled and thinly sliced	1
2	stalks lemongrass, smashed (see Tips, left)	2
1 tbsp	curry powder	15 mL
4	large mushrooms, quartered	4
1 lb	potatoes, peeled and diced	500 g
1 cup	boiling water	250 mL
8 oz	dry-style tofu (see Tips, left)	250 g
1	carrot, peeled and sliced	1
1	can (14 oz/400 mL) coconut milk	1
	Salt and freshly ground black pepper	
1	red bell pepper, seeded and chopped	1
½ cup	bean sprouts	125 mL

1. In a skillet or wok, heat oil over medium heat. Add shallots and stir-fry for 3 minutes, until softened. Add garlic, ginger, lemongrass and curry powder and stir-fry for 5 minutes, until fragrant. Add mushrooms and potatoes and stir-fry for 3 minutes. Add boiling water and stir, scraping up brown bits from bottom of pan.

2. Transfer to slow cooker stoneware. Add tofu, carrot and coconut milk. Season to taste with salt and freshly ground pepper. Cover and cook on High for 3 hours, until potatoes are tender. Stir in bell pepper. Cover and cook on High for 15 minutes, until pepper is tender.

3. *To serve:* Ladle the curry into large bowls and garnish each with a pile of bean sprouts.

Paneer & Pea Curry

Tip

Paneer is a fresh Indian cheese. It is available in South Asian markets. If you can't find it, substitute an equal quantity of pressed cottage cheese or firm tofu.

Preparation Time: 20 minutes
Medium (approx. 4 quart) slow cooker
Heat Rating: 🌶🌶

2 tbsp	oil	30 mL
8	shallots, finely chopped	8
1 tbsp	minced garlic	15 mL
2 tbsp	curry powder	30 mL
4	ripe plum tomatoes, coarsely chopped	4
2 tbsp	tomato paste	30 mL
2	long red chile peppers, thinly sliced	2
1 tsp	granulated sugar	5 mL
½ cup	water	125 mL
1 lb	paneer, cut into bite-size pieces (see Tip, left)	500 g
1 cup	table (18%) cream	250 mL
1½ cups	sweet green peas, thawed if frozen	375 mL
	Salt and freshly ground black pepper	
6 tbsp	finely chopped cilantro leaves	90 mL

1. In a large skillet or wok, heat oil over medium-high heat. Add shallots and stir-fry for 3 minutes, until softened. Add garlic and curry powder and stir-fry until fragrant, about 1 minute. Add tomatoes, tomato paste, chiles, sugar and water and stir well.

2. Transfer to slow cooker stoneware. Add paneer, cover and cook on High for 3 hours, until hot and bubbly. Add cream and peas. Cover and cook on High for 15 minutes, until peas are tender and flavors are melded. Season to taste with salt and freshly ground pepper. Stir in cilantro and serve immediately.

Spinach & Paneer Curry

Serves 4

Vegetarian Friendly

Tips

Serve with warm naan bread or hot rice.

To purée garlic and gingerroot use a fine, sharp-toothed grater, such as those made by Microplane.

Paneer is a fresh Indian cheese. It is available in South Asian markets. If you can't find it substitute an equal quantity of pressed cottage cheese or firm tofu.

Preparation Time: 20 minutes
Medium (approx. 4 quart) slow cooker
Heat Rating: 🌶🌶

¼ cup	ghee or butter	60 mL
1	onion, finely chopped	1
2 tsp	cumin seeds	10 mL
1 tbsp	puréed gingerroot (see Tips, left)	15 mL
2 tsp	puréed garlic	10 mL
1 tsp	cayenne	5 mL
1 tsp	ground coriander	5 mL
2	plum (Roma) tomatoes, finely chopped	2
8 oz	paneer, cut into bite-size pieces (see Tips, left)	250 g
	Salt and freshly ground black pepper	
1 lb	frozen spinach	500 g
2 tbsp	heavy or whipping (35%) cream	30 mL
1 tsp	freshly squeezed lemon juice	5 mL
2 tbsp	finely chopped cilantro leaves	30 mL

1. In a skillet or wok, melt ghee over medium-low heat. Add onion and cumin seeds and stir-fry until onion is lightly golden, about 8 minutes. Add ginger, garlic, cayenne and coriander and stir well. Stir in tomatoes.

2. Transfer to slow cooker stoneware. Add paneer and season to taste with salt and freshly ground pepper. Cover and cook on High for 3 hours, until hot and bubbly.

3. Meanwhile, bring a large saucepan of water to the boil. Add spinach and return to a boil. Cook for 3 minutes, then drain thoroughly. Transfer to a food processor fitted with the metal blade and blend to a smooth paste. Add cream and lemon juice and pulse to blend.

4. Add spinach mixture to stoneware and stir well. Cover and cook on High for 10 minutes to meld flavors. Garnish with cilantro and serve immediately.

Cashew Nut Curry

Tips

Serve this with rice and Indian pickles, if desired.

Screwpine (also known as pandanus) leaves are often used in Southeast Asian cooking. Look for them in Asian markets. You can use them fresh or frozen (thawed) or, if you prefer, substitute ½ tsp (2 mL) pandan paste in this recipe.

If you can't find galangal, substitute an equal quantity of puréed gingerroot.

To purée galangal and gingerroot, use a fine, sharp-toothed grater, such as those made by Microplane.

Preparation Time: 10 minutes
Medium (approx. 4 quart) slow cooker
Heat Rating: 🔥🔥

1	screwpine (pandanus) leaf (see Tips, left), shredded into thirds lengthwise and folded to fit stoneware	1
2 cups	coconut milk	500 mL
1 cup	raw cashew nuts	250 mL
1	onion, finely chopped	1
8	curry leaves	8
2	long green chile peppers, finely chopped	2
1	piece (4 inches/10 cm) cinnamon stick	1
1 tbsp	puréed gingerroot (see Tips, left)	15 mL
1 tsp	puréed galangal (see Tips, left)	5 mL
1 tsp	ground turmeric	5 mL
2 tbsp	chopped cilantro leaves	30 mL

1. Arrange screwpine leaf over bottom of slow cooker stoneware. Add coconut milk, cashews, onion, curry leaves, chiles, cinnamon stick, ginger, galangal and turmeric.

2. Cover and cook on Low for 6 to 8 hours, until nuts are tender. Remove and discard screwpine leaf and cinnamon stick. Garnish with cilantro and serve immediately.

South Indian Mango Curry

Serves 4

Vegan Friendly

Tips

As noted, this recipe is fiery. For a less incendiary dish, reduce the cayenne to ¼ to ½ tsp (1 to 2 mL). You might also consider reducing the quantity of fresh and/or dried chile peppers.

If you can't find curry leaves, substitute dried or fresh bay leaves.

Preparation Time: 20 minutes
Medium (approx. 4 quart) slow cooker
Heat Rating: 🌶🌶🌶

3	firm ripe mangoes, peeled, pitted and cut into bite-size pieces	3
1 tsp	ground turmeric	5 mL
1 tsp	cayenne pepper (see Tips, left)	5 mL
2 cups	water, divided	500 mL
2 cups	grated coconut, preferably fresh or frozen, thawed	500 mL
1 cup	coconut milk	250 mL
3	long green chile peppers, coarsely chopped	3
1 tbsp	cumin seeds	15 mL
¼ cup	oil	60 mL
2 tsp	black mustard seeds	10 mL
3	dried hot red chile peppers	3
12	curry leaves (see Tips, left)	12

1. In a saucepan, combine mangoes, turmeric, cayenne and 1 cup (250 mL) of the water. Bring to a boil over medium heat. Remove from heat and transfer to slow cooker stoneware.

2. In a food processor fitted with the metal blade, process coconut, coconut milk, green chiles, cumin seeds and remaining water until a fine paste forms. Add to slow cooker stoneware. Cover and cook on High for 3 hours.

3. In a small skillet, heat oil over medium-high heat. Add mustard seeds and cover. When the seeds stop popping, uncover and add dried chiles and curry leaves. Stir-fry for a few seconds, until the chiles darken. Add to mango curry and serve immediately.

Filipino Green Papaya Curry

Tips

When using canned coconut milk, be sure to shake well before using. The cream layer collects on the top after it's been sitting.

Coconut cream is a thicker, more concentrated version of coconut milk. Look for it in Asian markets. If you can't find it, skim off the top layer of a can of coconut milk that has been left standing.

Preparation time: 10 minutes
Medium (approx. 4 quart) slow cooker
Heat Rating:

2 tbsp	oil	30 mL
10	cloves garlic, minced	10
1	piece (1¾ inches/4 cm) peeled gingerroot, thinly sliced	1
10	black peppercorns	10
1 cup	coconut milk	250 mL
1	green papaya, peeled, seeded and thinly sliced	1
½ cup	boiling water	125 mL
	Salt	
1 cup	coconut cream (see Tips, left)	250 mL

1. In a large skillet or wok, heat oil over medium heat. Add garlic and stir-fry until lightly golden. Add ginger and peppercorns and stir-fry for 4 minutes. Stir in coconut milk.

2. Transfer to slow cooker stoneware. Add papaya and boiling water and season to taste with salt. Cover and cook on Low for 6 hours or on High for 3 hours, until papaya is translucent. Stir in coconut cream and serve immediately.

Nonya Laksa

Tips

Before chopping, remove and discard the tough outer layers of the lemongrass.

When using canned coconut milk, be sure to shake well before using. The cream layer collects on the top after it's been sitting.

Palm sugar is also known as jaggery. You can substitute raw cane sugar such as Mexican piloncillo, or regular dark brown sugar.

To hard-cook eggs: Place eggs in a single layer in a saucepan and cover with cold water. Cover and bring to a boil over high heat. Remove from heat and let stand for 10 minutes. Using a slotted spoon, transfer to a bowl of ice water. Cool for about 1 minute before peeling.

Preparation Time: 20 minutes
Medium (approx. 4 quart) slow cooker
Heat Rating: 🌶🌶

2 tbsp	oil	30 mL
2	onions, thinly sliced on the vertical	2
2 tbsp	finely chopped garlic	30 mL
1 tbsp	finely chopped lemongrass (see Tips, left)	15 mL
1 tbsp	minced gingerroot	15 mL
2	long red chile peppers, sliced	2
1/4 cup	medium curry powder	60 mL
1/2 tsp	ground turmeric	2 mL
1 1/4 cups	vegetable broth	300 mL
1	can (14 oz/400 mL) coconut milk	1
1 tsp	soft palm sugar (see Tips, left)	5 mL
8 oz	dried rice noodles	250 g

Accompaniments

4	green onions, thinly sliced	4
1 oz	finely chopped cilantro leaves	30 g
3	hard-cooked eggs, halved or quartered (see Tips, left)	3
2/3 cup	roasted skinless peanuts, coarsely chopped	150 mL
1/2 cup	bean sprouts	125 mL

1. In a large skillet or wok, heat oil over medium-high heat. Add onions and stir-fry for 3 minutes. Add garlic, lemongrass, ginger and chiles and stir-fry for 1 minute, until fragrant. Add curry powder and turmeric and stir well. Stir in vegetable broth, scraping up brown bits from bottom of pan.

2. Transfer to slow cooker stoneware. Add coconut milk and sugar and stir well. Cover and cook on High for 3 hours.

3. About half an hour before sauce has finished cooking, soak rice noodles in a large bowl of warm water until tender, about 20 minutes. Drain well. Divide noodles evenly among four warmed bowls and ladle laksa sauce evenly overtop. Serve immediately with accompaniments.

Rice & Pulses

Saffron Rice

Tips

This makes a wonderful accompaniment to any curry dish.

Be sure to use parboiled (also known as converted) rice. Because the process of parboiling keeps the kernels from sticking together, it works best in the slow cooker.

Preparation Time: 15 minutes
Small (2 to 3½ quart) slow cooker
Heat Rating:

1 tbsp	ghee or oil	15 mL
2	pieces (each 4 inches/10 cm) cinnamon stick	2
2	green cardamom pods	2
3	whole cloves	3
¼ tsp	ground turmeric	1 mL
2 tsp	saffron threads, soaked in 3 tbsp (45 mL) warm milk	10 mL
1 cup	long-grain parboiled (converted) white rice, preferably basmati	250 mL
2 cups	boiling water	500 mL
	Salt	

1. In a skillet or wok, heat ghee over medium heat. Add cinnamon, cardamom, cloves and turmeric and stir-fry for 30 seconds. Add saffron mixture and stir-fry for 30 seconds, until fragrant. Add rice and stir-fry until coated.

2. Transfer to slow cooker stoneware. Add boiling water and season to taste with salt. Cover and cook on Low for 3 hours, until liquid is absorbed and rice fluffs easily with a fork. Discard cinnamon, cardamom and cloves. Serve immediately.

Aromatic Pilaf

Serves 4

Vegan Friendly

Tip

This flavorful rice goes well with almost any curry dish.

Preparation time: 10 minutes
Small (2 to 3½ quart) slow cooker
Heat Rating:

2 tbsp	oil	30 mL
1	large onion, finely chopped	1
2	cloves garlic, minced	2
2 tsp	cumin seeds	10 mL
2	whole cloves	2
1 tsp	crushed cardamom pods	5 mL
2	pieces (each 4 inches/10 cm) cinnamon stick	2
1 tbsp	ground turmeric	15 mL
1 cup	long-grain parboiled (converted) white rice, preferably basmati	250 mL
2 cups	boiling water	500 mL
	Salt and freshly ground black pepper	
¼ cup	finely chopped cilantro leaves	60 mL

1. In a skillet or wok, heat oil over medium heat. Add onion and stir-fry until softened, about 3 minutes. Add garlic, cumin, cloves, cardamom, cinnamon and turmeric and stir-fry until fragrant, about 2 minutes. Add rice and stir-fry until coated.

2. Transfer to slow cooker stoneware. Add boiling water and season to taste with salt and freshly ground pepper. Cover and cook on Low for 3 hours, until liquid is absorbed and rice fluffs easily with a fork. Discard cloves and cinnamon. Stir in cilantro and serve immediately.

Mushroom Pilaf

Tip

Crisp-fried onions or shallots are available in many Asian markets. If you can't find a prepared version, you can make your own by stir-frying thinly sliced onions or shallots in an abundance of vegetable oil over medium-high heat, until they begin to brown. Lower the heat to medium and continue to stir-fry, watching carefully to ensure they don't burn, until crispy. Immediately transfer to a platter lined with paper towels to drain. It will take about 15 minutes.

Preparation Time: 10 minutes, plus soaking
Small (2 to 3½ quart) slow cooker
Heat Rating: ◊

1 cup	long-grain parboiled (converted) white rice, preferably basmati	250 mL
2 tbsp	oil	30 mL
8 oz	mushrooms, trimmed and sliced	250 g
1	piece (4 inches/10 cm) cinnamon stick	1
4	green cardamom pods, lightly crushed	4
2 tsp	cumin seeds	10 mL
8	black peppercorns	8
2	cloves	2
¼ cup	crisp-fried onions or shallots (see Tip, left)	60 mL
2 cups	boiling water	500 mL
	Salt and freshly ground black pepper	
1 cup	green peas, thawed if frozen	250 mL

1. Place rice in a bowl, cover with cold water and set aside to soak for 20 minutes. Drain thoroughly.

2. In a large skillet or wok, heat oil over high heat. Add mushrooms and stir-fry for 8 minutes. Add cinnamon, cardamom, cumin seeds, peppercorns and cloves and stir-fry until fragrant, about 2 minutes. Add crisp-fried onions and rice and toss to coat.

3. Transfer to slow cooker stoneware. Add boiling water and season to taste with salt and freshly ground pepper. Cover and cook on Low for 3 hours, until liquid is absorbed. Stir in peas. Cover and cook on High for 10 minutes, until heated through. Fluff up rice grains with a fork and serve immediately.

Green Bean & Carrot Pilaf

Tips

To purée gingerroot, use a fine, sharp-toothed grater, such as those made by Microplane.

If you don't like beans that are well-cooked, use sliced frozen (unthawed) beans in this recipe.

Preparation Time: 10 minutes, plus soaking
Small (2 to 3$\frac{1}{2}$ quart) slow cooker
Heat Rating:

1 cup	long-grain parboiled (converted) white rice, preferably basmati	250 mL
3 tbsp	ghee or oil	45 mL
2 tsp	mustard seeds	10 mL
2	large carrots, peeled and diced	2
1 cup	sliced green beans (see Tips, left)	250 mL
1	long red chile pepper, finely chopped	1
1 tbsp	puréed gingerroot (see Tips, left)	15 mL
1 tsp	ground turmeric	5 mL
1 tsp	garam masala	5 mL
2 cups	boiling water	500 mL

1. Wash rice in several changes of cold water. Drain well, place in a bowl and cover with fresh cold water. Set aside to soak for 30 minutes. Drain and transfer to slow cooker stoneware.

2. In a skillet or wok, heat ghee over medium-high heat. Add mustard seeds and cover. When the seeds stop popping, uncover, reduce heat to medium and add carrots, green beans, chile, ginger, turmeric and garam masala and stir-fry for 1 minute, until fragrant. Add to rice.

3. Stir in boiling water, cover and cook on Low for 3 hours, until liquid is absorbed. Fluff up rice grains with a fork and serve immediately.

Carrot & Pea Pilaf

Tips

For a quick main course, add cooked chicken or shrimp to the finished pilaf.

Be sure to use parboiled (also known as converted) rice. Because the process of parboiling keeps the kernels from sticking together, it works best in the slow cooker.

Preparation Time: 5 minutes, plus soaking
Small (2 to 3½ quart) slow cooker
Heat Rating: 🌶

1 cup	long-grain parboiled (converted) white rice, preferably basmati	250 mL
¼ cup	oil	60 mL
1	piece (2 inches/5 cm) cinnamon stick	1
2 tsp	cumin seeds	10 mL
2	cloves	2
4	green cardamom pods, lightly crushed	4
8	black peppercorns	8
1	large carrot, peeled and shredded	1
2 cups	boiling water	500 mL
	Salt and freshly ground black pepper	
1 cup	green peas, thawed if frozen	250 mL

1. Soak rice in a bowl of cold water for 30 minutes. Drain thoroughly and set aside.

2. In a skillet or wok, heat oil over medium heat. Add cinnamon, cumin, cloves, cardamom and peppercorns and stir-fry until fragrant. Add carrot and stir-fry for 2 minutes.

3. Transfer to slow cooker stoneware. Add reserved rice and boiling water and stir well. Season to taste with salt and freshly ground pepper. Cover and cook on Low for 3 hours. Stir in peas, cover and cook on High for 10 minutes, until tender. Fluff up rice with a fork and serve immediately.

Fava Bean Pilaf

Tip

To toast cumin seeds, place in a dry skillet over medium heat and stir-fry until fragrant, about 3 minutes. Immediately transfer to a small bowl and set aside.

Preparation Time: 10 minutes
Small (2 to 3½ quart) slow cooker
Heat Rating: ◊

1 cup	long-grain parboiled (converted) white rice, preferably basmati	250 mL
2 cups	shelled fava (broad) beans	500 mL
¼ cup	butter	60 mL
6	green onions, white and green parts, thinly sliced	6
1 tbsp	toasted cumin seeds (see Tip, left)	15 mL
2 cups	water	500 mL
	Salt and freshly ground black pepper	
6 tbsp	finely chopped dill fronds	90 mL
	Small handful of pomegranate seeds	

1. Wash rice in several changes of cold water until water runs clear. Drain and set aside.

2. Meanwhile, drop beans into a large pot of boiling water. Return to a boil and cook for 4 minutes. Drain in a colander, then transfer to a bowl of ice water. When cool, remove and discard the skins. Set beans aside.

3. In a skillet or wok, melt butter over low heat. Add green onions and cumin seeds and stir-fry for 2 minutes. Add rice and toss to coat.

4. Transfer to slow cooker stoneware. Stir in water and season to taste with salt and freshly ground pepper. Cover and cook on Low for 3 hours, until liquid is absorbed. Stir in fava beans and dill. Scatter pomegranate seeds evenly overtop. Serve immediately.

Burmese Golden Rice

Tips

This makes a wonderful accompaniment to any curry dish.

Be sure to use parboiled (also known as converted) rice. Because the process of parboiling keeps the kernels from sticking together, it works best in the slow cooker.

Preparation Time: 5 minutes
Small (2 to 3½ quart) slow cooker
Heat Rating: ♨

1 cup	long-grain parboiled (converted) white rice	250 mL
2 cups	boiling water	500 mL
2 tsp	ground turmeric	10 mL
1 tsp	saffron threads	5 mL
	Salt	
¼ cup	oil	60 mL
6	shallots, thinly sliced	6
8	cloves garlic, thinly sliced	8

1. In slow cooker stoneware, combine rice, boiling water, turmeric and saffron. Season to taste with salt and stir well. Cover and cook on Low for 3 hours, until liquid is absorbed.

2. Meanwhile, in a skillet, heat oil over medium-low heat. Add shallots and garlic and stir-fry until lightly browned and crisp, about 6 minutes. Drain on paper towels and set aside.

3. *To serve:* Using a fork, fluff up rice grains. Transfer to a deep platter and serve immediately, sprinkled with the fried shallots and garlic.

Coconut & Curry Leaf Rice

Tips

This rice is a great accompaniment for any curry dish.

If your main dish is quite spicy, you may want to reduce the quantity of chile peppers. One chile would produce a pleasantly hot rice.

Coconut cream is a thicker, more concentrated version of coconut milk. Look for it in Asian markets.

Preparation Time: 5 minutes, plus soaking
Small (2 to 3½ quart) slow cooker
Heat Rating: ♨♨

1 cup	long-grain parboiled (converted) white rice, preferably basmati	250 mL
2 tbsp	ghee or oil	30 mL
2 tsp	black mustard seeds	10 mL
10	curry leaves	10
2 tsp	cumin seeds	10 mL
2	dried red chile peppers, crumbled	2
2 cups	water	500 mL
½ cup	coconut cream	125 mL

1. Wash the rice in several changes of water, then soak for 15 minutes in a bowl of cold water. Drain thoroughly and transfer to slow cooker stoneware.

2. In a skillet or wok, heat ghee over medium-high heat. Add mustard seeds and cover. When the seeds stop popping, uncover, reduce heat to medium and add curry leaves, cumin seeds and chile peppers. Stir-fry until fragrant, about 1 minute. Add water and bring to a boil. Stir in coconut cream.

3. Transfer to slow cooker stoneware and stir well. Cover and cook on Low for 3 hours, until liquid is absorbed. Fluff up rice with a fork and serve immediately.

Yellow Rice with Chickpeas

Tips

If you don't like beans that are well-cooked, use sliced frozen (unthawed) beans in this recipe.

For this quantity of chickpeas, cook 1 cup (250 mL) dried chickpeas or use 1 can (14 to 19 oz/398 to 540 mL) chickpeas, drained and rinsed.

Preparation Time: 10 minutes, plus soaking
Small (2 to 3½ quart) slow cooker
Heat Rating: 🔥

1 cup	long-grain parboiled (converted) white rice, preferably basmati	250 mL
2 tbsp	oil	30 mL
1	onion, finely chopped	1
1	red bell pepper, seeded and cut into thin strips	1
1	clove garlic, minced	1
2 tsp	ground turmeric	10 mL
2 cups	cooked chickpeas (see Tips, left)	500 mL
1 cup	sliced green beans (see Tips, left)	250 mL
2 cups	boiling water	500 mL
	Salt and freshly ground black pepper	

1. Wash the rice in several changes of water, then soak for 15 minutes in a bowl of cold water. Drain thoroughly and set aside.

2. In a large skillet or wok, heat oil over medium heat. Add onion and stir-fry until soft, about 5 minutes. Add bell pepper and garlic and stir-fry for 2 minutes. Add turmeric and reserved rice and toss to coat.

3. Transfer to slow cooker stoneware. Add chickpeas, green beans and boiling water and stir well. Cover and cook on Low for 3 hours, until liquid is absorbed. Season to taste with salt and freshly ground pepper and serve immediately.

Tomato & Cilantro Rice

Serves 4

Vegan Friendly

Tip

Be sure to use parboiled (also known as converted) rice. Because the process of parboiling keeps the kernels from sticking together, it works best in the slow cooker.

Preparation Time: 20 minutes, plus soaking
Small (2 to 3½ quart) slow cooker
Heat Rating: ⚡

1 cup	long-grain parboiled (converted) white rice, preferably basmati	250 mL
3 tbsp	oil	45 mL
4	shallots, finely chopped	4
2	cloves garlic, finely chopped	2
2 tsp	cumin seeds	10 mL
4	ripe tomatoes, peeled and finely chopped, seeded if desired	4
	Salt and freshly ground black pepper	
2 cups	boiling water	500 mL
2 tbsp	finely chopped cilantro leaves	30 mL

1. Wash the rice in several changes of water, then soak for 15 minutes in a bowl of cold water. Drain thoroughly and set aside.

2. In a skillet or wok, heat oil over medium heat. Add shallots, garlic and cumin seeds and stir-fry until soft and fragrant, about 5 minutes. Add drained rice and toss to coat. Add tomatoes and stir-fry for 2 minutes.

3. Transfer to slow cooker stoneware. Season to taste with salt and freshly ground pepper. Add boiling water and stir well. Cover and cook on Low for 3 hours, until liquid is absorbed. Fluff up rice with a fork. Stir in cilantro and serve immediately.

Afghan-Style Fried Brown Rice

Serves 4

Vegan Friendly

Tip

Mace is the red skin that surrounds a nutmeg seed. If you can't find it, in this recipe substitute ½ tsp (2 mL) freshly grated nutmeg.

Preparation Time: 10 minutes, plus soaking
Small (2 to 3½ quart) slow cooker
Heat Rating: 🌶

1 cup	parboiled (converted) brown rice	250 mL
2 tbsp	ghee or oil	30 mL
2	onions, thinly sliced	2
1	piece (2 inches/5 cm) cinnamon stick	1
1	bay leaf	1
6	cloves	6
1	mace blade (see Tips, left)	1
1 tsp	granulated sugar	5 mL
	Salt	
2 cups	boiling water	500 mL

1. Place rice in a bowl and add 3 cups (750 mL) cold water. Set aside for 15 minutes. Rinse and drain well. Set aside.

2. In a skillet or wok, heat ghee over medium heat. Add onions and cook, stirring occasionally, until lightly browned and beginning to caramelize, about 15 minutes. Add cinnamon, bay leaf, cloves and mace and stir-fry for 5 minutes. Sprinkle sugar evenly overtop and stir-fry until onion mixture is golden brown, about 3 minutes.

3. Transfer to slow cooker stoneware. Add reserved rice and stir well. Season to taste with salt and add boiling water. Cover and cook on Low for 3 hours, until liquid is absorbed. Fluff up rice with a fork and serve immediately.

Spicy Vegetable Rice

Serves 4		
Vegan Friendly		

Tips

Serve in warmed bowls or plates.

To purée gingerroot, use a sharp-toothed grater such as those made by Microplane.

Preparation Time: 15 minutes
Small (2 to 3½ quart) slow cooker
Heat Rating: 🌶🌶🌶

1 tbsp	oil	15 mL
1	large red onion, finely chopped	1
2	cloves garlic, minced	2
2	long red chile peppers, minced	2
2 tsp	puréed gingerroot (see Tips, left)	10 mL
1 cup	parboiled (converted) rice, preferably basmati	250 mL
4	tomatoes, coarsely chopped	4
2 cups	boiling water	500 mL
2	yellow bell peppers, seeded and thinly sliced	2
2	red bell peppers, seeded and thinly sliced	2
1 cup	sliced okra	500 mL
¼ cup	finely chopped cilantro	60 mL

1. In a skillet or wok, heat oil over medium heat. Add onion, garlic, chiles and ginger and stir-fry for 5 minutes. Add rice and stir well. Add tomatoes and stir, scraping up brown bits from bottom of pan.

2. Transfer to slow cooker stoneware. Add boiling water, cover and cook on Low for 2½ hours.

3. Add bell peppers and okra. Cover and cook on High for about 30 minutes, until okra is tender and liquid is absorbed. Fluff up rice grains with a fork and garnish with cilantro.

Kitcheree

Tip

Be sure to use parboiled (also known as converted) rice. Because the process of parboiling keeps the kernels from sticking together, it works best in the slow cooker.

Preparation time: 15 minutes
Small (2 to 3½ quart) slow cooker
Heat Rating:

½ cup	split red lentils, picked over and rinsed	125 mL
3 tbsp	oil	45 mL
1	onion, finely chopped	1
1 tbsp	cumin seeds	15 mL
1 tsp	ground turmeric	5 mL
1	dried red chile pepper	1
1	piece (2 inches/5 cm) cinnamon stick	1
3	cloves	3
½ tsp	crushed cardamom seeds	2 mL
1 cup	long-grain parboiled (converted) white rice, preferably basmati, rinsed	250 mL
2¼ cups	boiling vegetable broth	550 mL
	Salt and freshly ground black pepper	
6 tbsp	finely chopped cilantro leaves	90 mL

Accompaniments

Assorted pickles
Poppadums or warm Indian bread (naan)
Plain yogurt

1. In a saucepan combine lentils and 2 cups (500 mL) cold water. Bring to a boil over high heat. Reduce heat and simmer for 10 minutes. Drain well and set aside.

2. In a skillet or wok, heat oil over medium heat. Add onion and stir-fry until very soft, about 5 minutes. Add cumin seeds, turmeric, chile, cinnamon stick, cloves and cardamom seeds and stir-fry for 2 minutes. Add rice and reserved drained lentils and stir-fry for 2 minutes.

3. Transfer to slow cooker stoneware. Add boiling broth and season to taste with salt and freshly ground pepper. Cover and cook on Low for 3 hours, until liquid is absorbed and rice is tender. Stir in cilantro. Serve immediately, with accompaniments.

Red Lentil Curry with Tamarind

Serves 4

Vegan Friendly

Tip

Be sure to use tamarind paste (sometimes labeled "concentrate"), which comes in a jar. Tamarind in a block needs to be dissolved in water and pressed through a sieve to remove seeds and pulp before being added to recipes and, therefore, becomes more diluted in flavor and texture.

Preparation Time: 10 minutes, plus soaking
Small (2 to 3½ quart) slow cooker
Heat Rating: ♨♨♨

1 cup	red lentils, picked over, rinsed and drained thoroughly	250 mL
6 cups	boiling water, divided	1.5 L
1 tsp	ground turmeric	5 mL
2 tbsp	oil	30 mL
1 tsp	black mustard seeds	5 mL
1 tbsp	curry powder	15 mL
4	dried red chile peppers	4
1	bay leaf	1
1 tbsp	soft palm sugar	15 mL
2 tsp	tamarind paste (see Tip, left)	10 mL
	Salt	

1. Place lentils in a bowl and add 3 cups (750 mL) of the boiling water. Set aside to soak for 1 hour, then drain thoroughly.

2. Transfer to slow cooker stoneware. Add turmeric and remaining 3 cups (750 mL) boiling water. Cover and cook on Low for 6 hours or on High for 3 hours, until lentils are tender. Using an immersion blender, purée until fairly smooth.

3. In a large skillet or wok, heat oil over medium-high heat. Add mustard seeds and cover. When the seeds stop popping, uncover, reduce heat to medium and add curry powder, chiles and bay leaf. Stir-fry until chiles darken in color, about 5 seconds. Stir in sugar and tamarind paste. Add cooked lentils, stir well and season to taste with salt. Mix well and serve immediately.

Creamy Spinach & Tomato Dhal

Serves 4

Vegan Friendly

Tips

Serve this with steamed basmati rice.

Fresh spinach can be gritty. Be sure to wash it thoroughly, preferably by swishing the leaves around in a basin of lukewarm water, then rinsing under cold running water.

Preparation Time: 10 minutes, plus soaking
Small (2 to 3½ quart) slow cooker
Heat Rating: ♦♦

1 cup	red lentils, picked over, rinsed and drained thoroughly	250 mL
5 cups	boiling water, divided	1.25 L
1¼ cups	coconut milk	300 mL
1 tsp	ground turmeric	5 mL
1 cup	spinach leaves, coarsely chopped	250 mL
4	tomatoes, coarsely chopped	4
	Small handful of finely chopped cilantro leaves	
2 tbsp	ghee or oil	30 mL
2 tbsp	minced garlic	30 mL
2 tbsp	minced gingerroot	30 mL
2	long red chile peppers, seeded and diced	2
1 tbsp	ground cumin	15 mL
2 tsp	cumin seeds	10 mL
2 tsp	ground coriander	10 mL
	Salt	

1. Place lentils in a bowl and cover with 3 cups (750 mL) of the boiling water. Set aside to soak for at least 1 hour or up to overnight. Drain and rinse well under cold running water.

2. Transfer drained lentils to slow cooker stoneware. Add remaining 2 cups (500 mL) boiling water and coconut milk and stir well. Stir in turmeric, spinach and tomatoes. Cover and cook on Low for 6 hours or on High for 3 hours, until lentils are tender. Whisk mixture until fairly smooth and stir in cilantro.

3. Meanwhile, in a small skillet, heat ghee over high heat. Add garlic, ginger, chiles, ground cumin, cumin seeds and ground coriander. Stir-fry until fragrant, about 40 seconds, then add to lentils. Stir well and season to taste with salt.

Masoor Dhal

Tips

Serve hot, with rice and pickles.

Crush the coriander seeds in a mortar with a pestle or place on a cutting board and use the bottom of a wine bottle.

Preparation Time: 10 minutes, plus soaking
Small (2 to 3½ quart) slow cooker
Heat Rating: ♨♨

1 cup	red lentils, picked over and rinsed	250 mL
6 cups	boiling water, divided	1.5 L
1 tsp	ground turmeric	5 mL
2 tbsp	oil	30 mL
1 tsp	black mustard seeds	5 mL
2 tbsp	curry powder	30 mL
2 tsp	cumin seeds	10 mL
1 tsp	crushed coriander seeds	5 mL
2	long green chile peppers, thinly sliced	2
10	curry leaves	10
4	cloves garlic, minced	4
1 tsp	minced gingerroot	5 mL
	Salt	

1. Place lentils in a bowl and add 3 cups (750 mL) of the boiling water. Set aside to soak for 1 hour. Drain thoroughly.

2. Transfer to slow cooker stoneware. Add remaining 3 cups (750 mL) boiling water and turmeric. Cover and cook on Low for 6 hours or on High for 3 hours, until lentils are tender. Using an immersion blender, purée until fairly smooth.

3. In a skillet or wok, heat oil over medium-high heat. Add mustard seeds and cover. When the seeds stop popping, uncover, reduce heat to medium and add curry powder, cumin and coriander seeds, chiles, curry leaves, garlic and ginger and stir-fry for 20 seconds. Add puréed lentil mixture and stir well. Season to taste with salt and serve immediately.

Sri Lankan Coconut Dhal

Serves 4

Vegan Friendly

Tips

Serve this dhal with rice or flatbread.

To whisk and roughly purée the cooked lentils, use a balloon whisk or an immersion blender.

Preparation Time: 15 minutes, plus soaking
Small (2 to 3½ quart) slow cooker
Heat Rating: ♨♨

1 cup	red lentils, picked over and rinsed	250 mL
3¼ cups	boiling water, divided	800 mL
2	shallots, finely chopped	2
2	ripe tomatoes, chopped	2
2	long green chile peppers, sliced	2
1 tsp	ground turmeric	5 mL
1	can (14 oz/400 mL) coconut milk	1
	Salt and freshly ground black pepper	
¼ cup	oil	60 mL
2 tsp	black mustard seeds	10 mL
1	onion, finely sliced	1
10	curry leaves	10

1. Place lentils in a bowl and add 2 cups (500 mL) of the boiling water. Set aside to soak for 1 hour, then drain thoroughly.

2. In slow cooker stoneware, combine lentils, shallots, tomatoes, chiles, turmeric and coconut milk. Stir well. Add remaining 1¼ cups (300 mL) boiling water and season to taste with salt and freshly ground pepper.

3. Cover and cook on Low for 6 hours or on High for 3 hours, until lentils are tender. Whisk until fairly smooth (see Tips, left).

4. In a skillet or wok, heat oil over medium-high heat. Add mustard seeds and cover. When the seeds stop popping, uncover, reduce heat to medium and add onion. Stir-fry until lightly browned, about 8 minutes. Add curry leaves and stir-fry until fragrant, about 1 minute. Pour spiced oil mixture over the lentils. Mix well and serve immediately.

Dhal Makhani

Tips

Serve this with rice and/or warm naan.

To purée gingerroot, use a fine, sharp-toothed grater, such as those made by Microplane.

For this quantity of beans, cook 1 cup (250 mL) dried red kidney beans or use 1 can (14 to 19 oz/398 to 540 mL), drained and rinsed.

Preparation Time: 40 minutes, plus soaking
Small (2 to 3½ quart) slow cooker
Heat Rating:

½ cup	whole black lentils, picked over	125 mL
4 cups	boiling water, divided	1 L
3 tbsp	ghee or butter	45 mL
1	onion, finely chopped	1
3	cloves garlic, minced	3
2 tsp	puréed gingerroot (see Tips, left)	10 mL
1	long green chile pepper, split in half lengthwise	1
2 tsp	cumin seeds	10 mL
1 tsp	ground coriander	5 mL
1 tsp	ground turmeric	5 mL
1 tsp	paprika, plus extra for sprinkling	5 mL
2 cups	cooked red kidney beans (see Tips, left)	500 mL
	Salt	
⅓ cup	chopped cilantro leaves	75 mL
¼ cup	table (18%) cream	60 mL

1. Place lentils in a deep bowl and cover with cold water. Set aside to soak for 12 hours. Transfer to a colander and rinse under cold running water. Drain.

2. In a saucepan, combine soaked lentils and 2 cups (500 mL) of the boiling water. Bring to a boil and cook for 20 minutes. Drain and set aside.

3. In a large skillet, melt ghee over medium heat. Add onion, garlic, ginger, chile, cumin and coriander and stir-fry until onion is soft and translucent. Add turmeric, paprika, kidney beans and reserved lentils and cook, stirring, for 2 minutes.

4. Transfer to slow cooker stoneware. Cover and cook on Low for 6 hours or on High for 3 hours, until lentils are tender. Season to taste with salt. Stir in cilantro and drizzle with cream. Sprinkle with paprika and serve immediately.

Tarka Dhal

Serves 4

Vegan Friendly

Tips

Serve with warm naan and rice.

Tarka is a mixture of herbs and spices cooked in oil and used to finish a dish. It is used in Indian cooking.

To whisk and roughly purée cooked lentils, use a balloon whisk or an immersion blender.

Preparation Time: 15 minutes, plus soaking
Small (2 to 3½ quart) slow cooker
Heat Rating: ◊

1 cup	split red lentils, picked over, rinsed and drained thoroughly	250 mL
6 cups	boiling water, divided	1.5 L
1 tsp	ground turmeric	5 mL
4	ripe tomatoes, coarsely chopped	4
	Salt and freshly ground black pepper	
⅓ cup	finely chopped cilantro leaves	75 mL

Tarka

¼ cup	oil	60 mL
2 tsp	black mustard seeds	10 mL
8	curry leaves	8
1 tbsp	cumin seeds	15 mL
2	cloves garlic, thinly sliced	2
2 tsp	minced gingerroot	10 mL
1	dried red chile pepper	1
2 tsp	ground cumin	10 mL
2 tsp	ground coriander	10 mL

1. In a bowl, combine lentils and 3 cups (750 mL) of the boiling water. Set aside to soak for 1 hour. Drain and transfer to slow cooker stoneware.

2. Add turmeric, tomatoes and remaining 3 cups (750 mL) boiling water. Cover and cook on Low for 6 hours or on High for 3 hours, until lentils are tender.

3. *Tarka:* In a skillet or wok, heat oil over medium-high heat. Add mustard seeds and cover. When the seeds stop popping, uncover, reduce heat to medium and add curry leaves, cumin seeds, garlic, ginger, chile, ground cumin and coriander and stir-fry until fragrant, about 2 minutes. Remove from heat.

4. When you are ready to serve, whisk cooked lentils until mixture is fairly smooth (see Tips, left). Season to taste with salt and freshly ground pepper and stir in the fresh cilantro. Pour tarka over mixture. Stir well and serve immediately.

Spiced Eggplant Dhal

Tips

Serve this with steamed basmati rice and/or an Indian bread such as naan.

To purée gingerroot, use a fine, sharp-toothed grater, such as those made by Microplane.

Peel the eggplant or leave the skin on, to suit your taste.

Preparation Time: 15 minutes, plus soaking
Small (2 to 3½ quart) slow cooker
Heat Rating: 🔥🔥

¾ cup	split yellow lentils, picked over and rinsed	175 mL
2 tbsp	oil	30 mL
1 tbsp	black mustard seeds	15 mL
2	onions, finely chopped	2
4	cloves garlic, minced	4
1 tsp	puréed gingerroot (see Tips, left)	5 mL
2 tbsp	curry powder	30 mL
1 tbsp	cumin seeds	15 mL
2 cups	water	500 mL
1	small eggplant, cut into bite-size cubes (see Tips, left)	1
8	cherry tomatoes	8
	Salt	
¼ cup	finely chopped cilantro	60 mL

1. Place lentils in a bowl and add boiling water to cover. Set aside for 1 hour. Drain thoroughly.

2. In a large skillet or wok, heat oil over medium-high heat. Add mustard seeds and cover. When the seeds stop popping, uncover, reduce heat to medium and add onions. Stir-fry until they start to turn golden, about 8 minutes. Add garlic, ginger, curry powder and cumin seeds and stir-fry until fragrant, about 2 minutes. Add water and bring to a boil, scraping up brown bits from bottom of pan.

3. Transfer to slow cooker stoneware. Add eggplant and cherry tomatoes. Cover and cook on Low for 6 hours or on High for 3 hours, until lentils are tender and dhal has thickened. Season to taste with salt and stir in cilantro. Serve immediately.

Sambhar

Tips

Serve this with plenty of hot rice.

As noted, this recipe is fiery. For a less incendiary dish, reduce the cayenne pepper to ¼ to ½ tsp (1 to 2 mL). You might also consider reducing the quantity of dried chiles.

Asafetida is a pungent powder with a garlic-like flavor that helps to make pulses more digestible. If you don't have it, in this recipe substitute ½ tsp (2 mL) each onion and garlic powder.

Preparation Time: 15 minutes, plus soaking
Small (2 to 3½ quart) slow cooker
Heat Rating: ♨♨♨

1 cup	split red lentils, picked over, rinsed and drained thoroughly	250 mL
6 cups	boiling water, divided	1.5 L
1 tsp	ground turmeric	5 mL
¼ cup	oil, divided	60 mL
1 tsp	black mustard seeds	5 mL
8	curry leaves	8
2	dried red chile peppers	2
½ tsp	fenugreek seeds	2 mL
1	onion, chopped	1
2	carrots, peeled and chopped	2
8 oz	green beans, cut into bite-size pieces (about 1½ cups/375 mL)	250 g
¼ cup	tamarind paste, dissolved in 1 cup (250 mL) hot water	60 mL
1	large tomato, finely chopped	1
¼ tsp	asafetida powder (see Tips, left)	1 mL

Sambhar Powder

1 tsp	ground coriander	5 mL
1 tsp	ground cumin	5 mL
1 tsp	cayenne pepper (see Tips, left)	5 mL
1 tsp	freshly ground black pepper	5 mL
½ tsp	black mustard seeds	2 mL
Pinch	ground cinnamon	Pinch
Pinch	ground cloves	Pinch

1. Place the lentils in a deep bowl and cover with 3 cups (750 mL) of the boiling water. Set aside to soak for at least 1 hour or up to overnight. When you're ready to cook, drain and rinse well under cold running water.

2. Transfer to slow cooker stoneware. Add remaining 3 cups (750 mL) boiling water, turmeric and 2 tbsp (30 mL) of the oil. Cover and cook on Low for 6 hours or on High for 3 hours, until lentils are very soft.

Tip

To whisk and roughly purée cooked lentils, use a balloon whisk or an immersion blender.

3. When lentils have almost finished cooking, in a skillet or wok, heat remaining 2 tbsp (30 mL) oil over medium-high heat. Add 1 tsp (5 mL) mustard seeds and cover. When the seeds stop popping, uncover, reduce heat to medium and add curry leaves, chiles and fenugreek and stir-fry for 2 minutes. Add onion and carrots and stir-fry until softened, about 5 minutes. Add green beans and tamarind mixture and bring to a boil. Cook until beans are tender-crisp, about 4 minutes. Stir in tomato and remove from heat. Stir in asafetida.

4. *Sambhar Powder:* Meanwhile, in a small bowl, combine coriander, cumin, cayenne, black pepper, $1/2$ tsp (2 mL) mustard seeds, cinnamon and cloves.

5. Whisk cooked lentils until they form a coarse purée (see Tip, left). Add bean mixture and sambhar powder. Stir well and serve immediately.

Saag Dhal

Serves 4

Vegan Friendly

Tip

Serve this dhal with steamed basmati rice or a warm Indian bread such as naan or chapatti.

Preparation Time: 10 minutes, plus soaking
Small (2 to 3½ quart) slow cooker
Heat Rating: ♨♨

1 cup	yellow split peas, picked over and rinsed	250 mL
6 cups	boiling water, divided	1.5 L
1 tsp	ground turmeric	5 mL
15	cherry tomatoes	15
1 cup	baby spinach, coarsely chopped	250 mL
¼ cup	finely chopped cilantro leaves	60 mL
2 tbsp	ghee or oil	30 mL
2 tsp	black mustard seeds	10 mL
2 tbsp	minced garlic	30 mL
2 tbsp	minced gingerroot	30 mL
2	long green chile peppers, seeded and finely sliced	2
1 tbsp	ground coriander	15 mL
1 tbsp	ground cumin	15 mL
2 tsp	cumin seeds	10 mL
	Salt	

1. Place split peas in a bowl and cover with 3 cups (750 mL) of the boiling water. Set aside to soak for at least 1 hour or up to overnight. When you're ready to cook, drain and rinse under cold running water.

2. Transfer to slow cooker stoneware. Add turmeric, cherry tomatoes and remaining 3 cups (750 mL) boiling water. Cover and cook on Low for 6 to 8 hours or on High for 3 to 4 hours, until lentils are tender. Stir in spinach. Cover and cook on High for 10 minutes, until spinach is wilted. Whisk mixture until fairly smooth. Stir in cilantro.

3. In a small skillet, heat ghee over medium-high heat. Add mustard seeds and cover. When the seeds stop popping, uncover, reduce heat to medium and add garlic, ginger, chiles, coriander, ground cumin and cumin seeds. Stir-fry until fragrant, about 40 seconds. Add to lentil mixture. Mix well and season to taste with salt. Serve immediately.

Kali Dhal

Tips

To purée gingerroot, use a fine, sharp-toothed grater, such as those made by Microplane.

For this quantity of beans, cook ½ cup (125 mL) dried red kidney beans or use about half of a standard can (14 to 19 oz/398 to 540 mL), drained and rinsed.

Preparation Time: 40 minutes, plus soaking
Small (2 to 3½ quart) slow cooker
Heat Rating: ♨♨

½ cup	dried whole black lentils, picked over and rinsed	125 mL
4 cups	boiling water, divided	1 L
3 tbsp	ghee or butter	45 mL
1	onion, finely chopped	1
3	cloves garlic, minced	3
2 tsp	puréed gingerroot (see Tips, left)	10 mL
2	long green chile peppers, split in half lengthwise	2
1 tbsp	ground cumin	15 mL
1 tbsp	ground coriander	15 mL
1 tsp	ground turmeric	5 mL
1 tsp	sweet paprika, plus extra for sprinkling	5 mL
1 cup	cooked red kidney beans (see Tips, left)	250 mL
	Salt	
⅓ cup	chopped cilantro leaves	75 mL
½ cup	heavy or whipping (35%) cream	125 mL

1. Place lentils in a bowl and add cold water to cover. Set aside for 12 hours to soak. Drain and rinse under cold running water. Place in a saucepan with 2 cups (500 mL) of the boiling water. Cover and simmer for 20 minutes. Drain and set aside.

2. In a skillet or wok, melt ghee over medium heat. Add onion, garlic, ginger and chiles and stir-fry for 6 minutes, until onion is soft and translucent. Add cumin, coriander, turmeric and paprika and stir-fry for 1 minute, until fragrant. Add kidney beans and reserved lentils and stir well.

3. Transfer to slow cooker stoneware. Add remaining 2 cups (500 mL) boiling water. Cover and cook on Low for 6 hours or on High for 3 hours, until hot and bubbly. Season to taste with salt. Stir in chopped cilantro, drizzle with cream and sprinkle with additional paprika.

Spiced Chickpea Curry

Tips

Serve this with steamed rice and/or an Indian bread such as naan.

As noted, this recipe is fiery. For a less incendiary dish, reduce the cayenne pepper to ¼ to ½ tsp (1 to 2 mL).

For this quantity of chickpeas, cook 1 cup (250 mL) dried chickpeas or use 1 can (14 to 19 oz/398 to 540 mL) chickpeas, drained and rinsed.

Preparation Time: 20 minutes
Small (2 to 3½ quart) slow cooker
Heat Rating: 🌶🌶🌶

2 tbsp	oil	30 mL
2	onions, thinly sliced on the vertical	2
1 tbsp	curry powder	15 mL
2 tsp	ground coriander	10 mL
2 tsp	ground cumin	10 mL
1 tsp	cayenne pepper (see Tips, left)	5 mL
½ tsp	ground turmeric	2 mL
½ cup	water	125 mL
2 cups	cooked chickpeas (see Tips, left)	500 mL
1	can (14 oz/398 mL) diced tomatoes, with juice	1
1 tsp	brown sugar	5 mL
	Salt and freshly ground black pepper	
2 tbsp	chopped mint leaves	30 mL
1 cup	baby spinach leaves	250 mL
½ cup	plain yogurt, lightly whisked	125 mL

1. In a skillet or wok, heat oil over low heat. Add onions and cook, stirring occasionally, until lightly golden, about 15 minutes. Add curry powder, coriander, cumin, cayenne and turmeric and stir-fry until fragrant, about 2 minutes. Add water and stir well.

2. Transfer to slow cooker stoneware. Stir in chickpeas, tomatoes, with juice, and sugar. Season to taste with salt and freshly ground black pepper. Cover and cook on Low for 6 hours or on High for 3 hours, until mixture is hot and bubbly. Stir in mint.

3. To serve, divide spinach evenly among four shallow bowls and top with chickpea mixture. Drizzle with yogurt and serve immediately.

Spiced Red Kidney Bean Curry

Serves 4

Vegetarian Friendly

Tips

To purée gingerroot, use a sharp-toothed grater such as those made by Microplane.

For this quantity of kidney beans, cook 1 cup (250 mL) dried red kidney beans or use 1 can (14 to 19 oz/398 to 540 mL) red kidney beans, drained and rinsed.

Preparation Time: 10 minutes
Small (2 to 3½ quart) slow cooker
Heat Rating: ♨♨

2 tbsp	oil	30 mL
1	onion, finely chopped	1
1	piece (2 inches/5 cm) cinnamon stick	1
4	cloves garlic, minced	4
2 tsp	puréed gingerroot (see Tips, left)	10 mL
2	dried bay leaves	2
2 tbsp	mild or medium curry powder	30 mL
2 tsp	ground cumin	10 mL
1 tsp	ground coriander	5 mL
1	can (14 oz/398 mL) diced tomatoes, with juice	1
2 cups	cooked red kidney beans, (see Tips, left)	500 mL
1 cup	boiling water	250 mL
	Salt and freshly ground black pepper	
	Plain yogurt, whisked	
	Chopped cilantro leaves	

1. In a skillet or wok, heat oil over medium heat. Add onion, cinnamon, garlic, ginger and bay leaves and stir-fry for 5 minutes. Stir in curry powder, cumin and coriander. Add tomatoes and bring to a boil, stirring and scraping up brown bits from bottom of pan.

2. Transfer to slow cooker stoneware. Add kidney beans and boiling water. Cover and cook on Low for 6 hours or on High for 3 hours, until hot and bubbly. Season to taste with salt and freshly ground pepper. Just before serving, stir in whisked yogurt and chopped cilantro to taste.

Channa Masala

Serves 4

Vegetarian Friendly

Tips

Use the large holes on a box grater to grate the onion.

If you prefer milder spicing, use one chile and reduce the quantity of cayenne pepper to $\frac{1}{2}$ tsp (2 mL).

Be sure to use tamarind paste (sometimes labeled "concentrate"), which comes in a jar. Tamarind in a block needs to be dissolved in water and pressed through a sieve to remove seeds and pulp before being added to recipes and, therefore, becomes more diluted in flavor and texture.

For this quantity of chickpeas, cook 1 cup (250 mL) dried chickpeas or use 1 can (14 to 19 oz/398 to 540 mL) chickpeas, drained and rinsed.

Preparation Time: 10 minutes
Small (2 to 3½ quart) slow cooker
Heat Rating: ♨♨

2 tbsp	oil	30 mL
1	large onion, coarsely grated (see Tips, left)	1
4	cloves garlic, minced	4
2 tsp	puréed gingerroot	10 mL
1 to 2	long green chile peppers, thinly sliced	1 to 2
1 tbsp	ground cumin	15 mL
1 tbsp	ground coriander	15 mL
2 tsp	curry powder	10 mL
2 tsp	garam masala	10 mL
1 tsp	cayenne pepper (see Tips, left)	5 mL
3 tbsp	plain yogurt (not lower-fat)	45 mL
2 tsp	tamarind paste (see Tips, left)	10 mL
2 cups	boiling water	500 mL
2 cups	cooked chickpeas (see Tips, left)	500 mL
	Chopped cilantro leaves	
	Plain yogurt, whisked	
	Lemon wedges	

1. In a large skillet or wok, heat oil over medium heat. Add onion, garlic, ginger and chile(s) and stir-fry until onion is turning golden, about 8 minutes. Add cumin, coriander, curry powder, garam masala and cayenne and stir-fry for 2 minutes, until fragrant. Stir in yogurt and tamarind paste. Add water and stir, scraping up brown bits from bottom of pan.

2. Transfer to slow cooker stoneware and stir in chickpeas. Cover and cook on Low for 6 hours or on High for 3 hours, until hot and bubbly. Garnish with cilantro and drizzle with whisked yogurt. Serve immediately, with lemon wedges on the side.

Accompaniments

Sweet Mango Chutney

Tips

Serve this chutney with any Indian curry and rice.

To sterilize canning jars, immerse in a pot of simmering, not boiling, water for 10 minutes or wash using the sterilizing cycle in the dishwasher. Keep hot until filling.

Preparation Time: 20 minutes
Small (approx. 1½ to 3 quart) slow cooker
Heat Rating:

1 tbsp	oil	15 mL
1 tsp	puréed gingerroot	5 mL
2	cloves garlic, minced	2
1 tbsp	nigella seeds	15 mL
½ tsp	cayenne pepper	2 mL
5	cloves	5
5	black peppercorns	5
2	pieces (each about 2 inches/5 cm) cinnamon stick	2
1	star anise	1
3½ cups	chopped peeled mango	875 mL
1⅔ cups	white wine vinegar	400 mL
1¼ cups	granulated sugar	300 mL
	Salt	

1. In a saucepan, heat oil over medium heat. Add ginger, garlic, nigella seeds, cayenne, cloves, peppercorns, cinnamon and star anise and stir-fry until fragrant, about 2 minutes. Add mango, vinegar and sugar. Bring to a boil, stirring gently until sugar has dissolved.

2. Transfer to slow cooker stoneware. Cover and cook on Low for 6 to 8 hours, until mixture is thickened. Season to taste with salt.

3. Meanwhile, sterilize canning jar (see Tips, left). Empty water from jar and fill with chutney. Seal jar with tight-fitting lid and refrigerate for at least three days. Store in the refrigerator for up to three weeks.

Apple & Mango Chutney

Tips

Choose a firm apple that holds its shape when cooked, such as Granny Smith.

When cooking is completed, your chutney may not be as thick as it would be if cooked on the stovetop. However, the texture improves upon refrigeration.

To sterilize canning jars, immerse in a pot of simmering, not boiling, water for 10 minutes or wash using the sterilizing cycle in the dishwasher. Keep hot until filling.

Preparation Time: 10 minutes
Small (approx. 3 quart) slow cooker
Heat Rating: 🌶🌶

1 tbsp	oil	15 mL
1	onion, halved lengthwise and thinly sliced	1
1 tsp	puréed gingerroot	5 mL
1	piece (2 inches/5 cm) cinnamon stick	1
½ tsp	coriander seeds, crushed	2 mL
¼ tsp	cardamom seeds, crushed	1 mL
¼ tsp	nigella seeds	1 mL
1	cooking apple, peeled, cored and coarsely chopped (see Tips, left)	1
1⅔ cups	chopped peeled mango	400 mL
1	long red chile pepper, finely chopped	1
1 tsp	ground turmeric	5 mL
⅔ cup	white wine vinegar	150 mL
¾ cup	granulated sugar	175 mL
¾ cup	boiling water	175 mL
	Salt	

1. In a saucepan, heat oil over medium heat. Add onion and stir-fry until softened, about 3 minutes. Add ginger and stir-fry until onion is golden, about 8 minutes. Stir in cinnamon and coriander, cardamom and nigella seeds and stir-fry for 2 minutes.

2. Transfer to slow cooker stoneware. Add apple, mango, chile, turmeric, vinegar and sugar. Add boiling water and season to taste with salt. Cover and cook on Low for 6 to 8 hours or until mixture is thickened (see Tips, left).

3. Meanwhile, sterilize canning jars (see Tips, left). Empty water from jars and fill with chutney. Seal jars with tight-fitting lids and refrigerate for at least one week. Store in the refrigerator for up to one month.

Pineapple Chutney

Tips

Serve with any Indian curry and rice.

To sterilize canning jars, immerse in a pot of simmering, not boiling, water for 10 minutes or wash using the sterilizing cycle in the dishwasher. Keep hot until filling.

Preparation Time: 20 minutes
Small (approx. 1 to 3 quart) slow cooker
Heat Rating:

1 tbsp	oil	15 mL
2 tbsp	coriander seeds	30 mL
2	pieces (each 2 inches/5 cm) cinnamon stick	2
1 tsp	puréed gingerroot	5 mL
5	cloves	5
5	black peppercorns	5
2 cups	ripe but firm pineapple chunks (1 inch/2.5 cm)	500 mL
1$\frac{2}{3}$ cups	white wine vinegar	400 mL
1$\frac{1}{3}$ cups	packed light brown sugar	325 mL
	Salt	

1. In a saucepan, heat oil over medium heat. Add coriander, cinnamon, cayenne, ginger, cloves and peppercorns and stir-fry until fragrant, about 2 minutes. Add pineapple, vinegar and sugar and bring to a boil. Cook, stirring gently, until sugar dissolves.

2. Transfer to slow cooker stoneware. Cover and cook on Low for 6 to 8 hours, until thickened. Season to taste with salt.

3. Meanwhile, sterilize canning jar (see Tips, left). Empty water from jar and fill with chutney. Seal jar with tight-fitting lid and refrigerate for at least three days. Store in the refrigerator for up to one month.

Spiced Beet & Apple Chutney

Makes about three 1-pint (500 mL) jars

Vegan Friendly

Tips

Choose a firm apple that holds its shape when cooked, such as Granny Smith.

When cooking is completed, your chutney may not be as thick as it would be if cooked on the stovetop. However, the texture improves upon refrigeration.

To sterilize canning jars, immerse in a pot of simmering, not boiling, water for 10 minutes or wash using the sterilizing cycle in the dishwasher. Keep hot until filling.

Preparation Time: 10 minutes
Small (approx. 3 quart) slow cooker
Heat Rating: ◊

3	onions, finely chopped	3
1 lb	trimmed beets, cooked, peeled and finely chopped	500 g
2	firm cooking apples, peeled, cored and finely chopped (see Tips, left)	2
1⅓ cups	packed brown sugar	325 mL
1 cup	white vinegar	250 mL
1 tbsp	crushed coriander seeds	15 mL
1 tbsp	crushed cumin seeds	15 mL
2 tsp	salt	10 mL

1. In slow cooker stoneware, combine onions, beets, apples, sugar, vinegar, coriander and cumin seeds and salt. Cover and cook on Low for 6 to 8 hours, until thickened.

2. Meanwhile, sterilize canning jars (see Tips, left). Empty water from jars and fill with chutney. Seal jars with tight-fitting lids and refrigerate for at least three days. Store in the refrigerator for up to two weeks. Bring to room temperature before serving.

Chile & Tomato Chutney

Tips

Serve this fiery chutney with any curry and rice dish that might welcome a hit of spice.

To purée gingerroot, use a fine, sharp-toothed grater, such as those made by Microplane.

This produces a very spicy chutney. If you prefer a less incendiary version, reduce the quantity of chile flakes.

To sterilize canning jars, immerse in a pot of simmering, not boiling, water for 10 minutes or wash using the sterilizing cycle in the dishwasher. Keep hot until filling.

Preparation Time: 10 minutes
Small (approx. 1 to 3 quart) slow cooker
Heat Rating: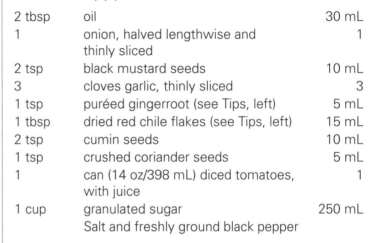

2 tbsp	oil	30 mL
1	onion, halved lengthwise and thinly sliced	1
2 tsp	black mustard seeds	10 mL
3	cloves garlic, thinly sliced	3
1 tsp	puréed gingerroot (see Tips, left)	5 mL
1 tbsp	dried red chile flakes (see Tips, left)	15 mL
2 tsp	cumin seeds	10 mL
1 tsp	crushed coriander seeds	5 mL
1	can (14 oz/398 mL) diced tomatoes, with juice	1
1 cup	granulated sugar	250 mL
	Salt and freshly ground black pepper	

1. In a skillet, heat oil over medium-high heat. Add onion and stir-fry until lightly browned, about 7 minutes. Add mustard seeds and cover. When the seeds stop popping, uncover, reduce heat to medium and add garlic, ginger, chile flakes, cumin and coriander and stir-fry for 3 minutes. Add tomatoes and sugar and stir well.

2. Transfer to slow cooker stoneware. Season to taste with salt and freshly ground pepper. Cover and cook on Low for 6 hours, until slightly thickened.

3. Meanwhile, sterilize canning jar (see Tips, left). Empty water from jar and fill with chutney. Seal jar with tight-fitting lid and refrigerate for at least three days. Store in the refrigerator for up to one week. Bring to room temperature before serving.

Indian Red Cabbage Chutney

Makes about two 1-pint (500 mL) jars

Vegan Friendly

Tips

This quantity of hot pepper flakes produces a pleasantly peppery chutney. One teaspoon (5 mL) of cayenne will produce a ♦♦♦ result.

When cooking is completed, your chutney may not be as thick as it would be if cooked on the stovetop. However, the texture improves upon refrigeration.

Preparation Time: 15 minutes
Small (approx. 3 quart) slow cooker
Heat Rating: ◊

3 cups	shredded red cabbage (about 12 oz/ 375 g)	750 mL
2	apples, peeled, cored and finely chopped	2
1 tbsp	minced gingerroot	15 mL
3	cloves garlic, minced	3
2 tsp	hot pepper flakes or 1 tsp (5 mL) cayenne pepper (see Tips, left)	10 mL
1 tsp	ground turmeric	5 mL
1	piece (2 inches/5 cm) cinnamon stick	1
1 cup	packed brown sugar	250 mL
1 cup	red wine vinegar	250 mL

1. In slow cooker stoneware, combine cabbage, apples, ginger, garlic, pepper flakes, turmeric, cinnamon, brown sugar and vinegar. Cover and cook on Low for 6 to 8 hours, until cabbage is tender and mixture has thickened (see Tips, left.)

2. Meanwhile, sterilize canning jars (see Tips, page 180). Empty water from jars and fill with chutney. Seal jars with tight-fitting lids and refrigerate for at least three days. Store in the refrigerator for up to three weeks.

Spiced Carrot Pickle

Tips

As noted, this produces a very spicy pickle. If you prefer a milder result, reduce the quantity of cayenne and/or fresh chile peppers.

To sterilize canning jars, immerse in a pot of simmering, not boiling, water for 10 minutes or wash using the sterilizing cycle in the dishwasher. Keep hot until filling.

Preparation Time: 15 minutes
Small (approx. 3 quart) slow cooker
Heat Rating: ♨♨♨

1 lb	trimmed carrots, peeled and cut into 2-inch (5 cm) sticks	500 g
7 oz	small shallots, preferably Thai, peeled but left whole	210 g
6	long green chile peppers	6
2/3 cup	white wine vinegar	150 mL
3/4 cup	water	175 mL
1 tsp	salt	5 mL
1/2 tsp	ground turmeric	2 mL

Pickling Paste

2/3 cup	white wine vinegar	150 mL
1 tbsp	black mustard seeds	15 mL
1 tbsp	granulated sugar	15 mL
4	cloves garlic, minced	4
2 tsp	puréed gingerroot	10 mL
2 tsp	cayenne pepper (see Tips, left)	10 mL
	Salt	

1. In slow cooker stoneware, combine carrots, shallots, chiles, vinegar and water. Sprinkle salt and turmeric evenly overtop. Cover and cook on High for 3 hours. Drain, discarding cooking liquid. Set vegetables aside.

2. *Pickling Paste:* In a food processor fitted with the metal blade, process vinegar, mustard seeds, sugar, garlic, ginger and cayenne until a smooth paste forms. Season to taste with salt and pulse to blend. Transfer to a bowl. Add drained vegetables and toss to coat evenly.

3. Meanwhile, sterilize canning jars (see Tips, left). Empty water from jars and fill with chutney. Seal jars with tight-fitting lids and refrigerate for at least three days. Store in the refrigerator for up to one month.

Burmese Cucumber Pickle

Makes about 3½ cups (875 mL)

Vegan Friendly

Tip

To toast sesame seeds, place in a dry skillet over medium heat and stir-fry until they begin to brown. Immediately transfer to a small bowl and set aside.

Preparation Time: 10 minutes
Small (approx. 3 quart) slow cooker
Heat Rating:

2	large cucumbers, peeled and halved lengthwise, seeds removed	2
1 cup	boiling water	250 mL
½ cup	malt vinegar	125 mL
1 tsp	salt	5 mL
¼ cup	peanut oil	60 mL
2 tbsp	light sesame oil	30 mL
8	cloves garlic, thinly sliced	8
1	onion, halved lengthwise and thinly sliced	1
2 tbsp	toasted sesame seeds	30 mL

1. On a cutting board, cut cucumber lengthwise into ½-inch (1 cm) strips, then cut strips crosswise into 2-inch (5 cm) pieces, if necessary.

2. Transfer to slow cooker stoneware. Add boiling water, vinegar and salt. Cover and cook on Low for 6 hours, until cucumber is translucent. Drain and set aside to cool, discarding liquid.

3. In a skillet, heat peanut and sesame oils over medium heat. Add garlic and stir-fry until pale golden, about 3 minutes. Remove with a slotted spoon and drain on paper towels. Add onion to pan and stir-fry until lightly browned, about 8 minutes.

4. In a serving dish, combine cooled cucumber, fried garlic and onion, including the oil from the pan, and toasted sesame seeds. Serve immediately.

Library and Archives Canada Cataloguing in Publication

Vijayakar, Sunil
    150 best Indian, Thai, Vietnamese & more slow cooker recipes / Sunil Vijayakar.

Includes index.
ISBN 978-0-7788-0404-8

1. Electric cooking, Slow. 2. Cooking, Indic. 3. Cooking, Vietnamese. 4. Cooking, Thai.
5. Cookbooks. I. Title. II. Title: One hundred fifty best Indian, Thai, Vietnamese and more
slow cooker recipes.

TX827.V55 2012   641.5'884   C2011-907396-X

Index